ENGLISH REVIEW MANUAL

A PROGRAM FOR SELF-INSTRUCTION

Third Edition

James A. Gowen
University of Kansas

CHAMPLAIN COLLEGE

McGraw-Hill Book Company

New York St. Louis San Francisco Auckland Bogotá Hamburg
Johannesburg London Madrid Mexico Montreal New Delhi
Panama Paris São Paulo Singapore Sydney Tokyo Toronto

This book was set in Palatino by Intergraphic Technology, Inc.
The editors were William A. Talkington and Barry Benjamin;
the designer was Joan E. O'Connor;
the production supervisor was Donna Piligra.
R. R. Donnelley & Sons Company was printer and binder.

ENGLISH REVIEW MANUAL
A Program for Self-Instruction

1 2 3 4 5 6 7 8 9 0   DODO   8 9 8 7 6 5 4 3 2 1 0

Library of Congress Cataloging in Publication Data

Gowen, James A
   English review manual.

   Bibliography: p.
   Includes index.
   1. English language—Grammar—1950-   —Programmed instruction. I. Title.
PE1112.5.G6 1980   428'.2   79-18299
ISBN 0-07-023895-2

ENGLISH REVIEW MANUAL

A PROGRAM FOR SELF-INSTRUCTION

Third Edition

James A. Gowen
University of Kansas

McGraw-Hill Book Company

New York St. Louis San Francisco Auckland Bogotá Hamburg
Johannesburg London Madrid Mexico Montreal New Delhi
Panama Paris São Paulo Singapore Sydney Tokyo Toronto

This book was set in Palatino by Intergraphic Technology, Inc.
The editors were William A. Talkington and Barry Benjamin;
the designer was Joan E. O'Connor;
the production supervisor was Donna Piligra.
R. R. Donnelley & Sons Company was printer and binder.

ENGLISH REVIEW MANUAL
A Program for Self-Instruction

1 2 3 4 5 6 7 8 9 0   DODO   8 9 8 7 6 5 4 3 2 1 0

Library of Congress Cataloging in Publication Data

Gowen, James A
   English review manual.

   Bibliography: p.
   Includes index.
   1. English language—Grammar—1950-   —Programmed
instruction. I. Title.
PE1112.5.G6 1980   428'.2   79-18299
ISBN 0-07-023895-2

CONTENTS

PREFACE

This book offers a thorough review of the principles and conventions of written English. Its plan allows students to study independently, using the text according to their particular needs. Primarily designed to help composition teachers minimize the expense of classroom time on the principles of grammatical usage, the book is also suited to courses dealing exclusively with usage problems. In addition, students not enrolled in English courses will find it a convenient guide for independent study.

This book is a proved equivalent of intensive initial units dealing with usage problems in college composition courses. By assigning it for parallel study to replace such units, a teacher can concentrate from the beginning of the course on the more important aspects of composition—organization, paragraphing, diction, tone, style, and the rest. In courses focused primarily on usage, it can serve as a basic text for an entire term.

An instructor's manual is available on request. It contains a detailed explanation of the book's structure and suggestions for using the text in different kinds of courses, together with a series of tests—diagnostic and final tests as well as progress tests covering parts of the book. It also contains additional exercise material for each unit. The instructor's manual is designed so that the test and exercise material may easily be converted to Thermofax spirit masters or transparencies.

A NOTE ON THE THIRD EDITION

The interest that *English Review Manual* has had since the publication of its first edition in 1965 has been gratifying. It was conceived of as a review and reference text for students who had a significant amount of English in prior courses; but it has also proved effective for students with weak backgrounds, who have found it an effective guide for making up lost ground in their study of written English. The second edition, published in 1970, maintained the same structure and general content but included more material and clarification of areas in which students who had used the text reported difficulty.

This, the third edition, is modified in two basic ways. While it remains a review and reference text, with its integrated express-stopping structure, this new edition has a simplified system of grammatical analysis, linked directly to the related usage problems; and greater stress falls on those problems that have proved to be of most difficulty to most students. Along with these basic changes, certain more specialized issues of usage and outdated forms of grammatical analysis have been dropped. These modifications reflect an effort to make the text more accessible and hence more useful to students enrolled in composition courses at the present time, whose backgrounds in a large measure differ from those of students of the decade past. However, those who have used earlier editions will recognize much that is familiar, since those portions that experience with the text has shown to be successful have been retained.

I would like to thank Tina Blue, who provided some new material for this edition as well as some valuable suggestions for sequencing of its parts. For their editorial suggestions on the third edition, I would like also to thank Warren H. Chelline, Missouri Western State College; Don Duffy, Central State University; and Joseph LaFay, University of Syracuse.

I would especially like to thank Barbara Paris, whose help in all stages of the preparation of this edition I could not have done without.

James A. Gowen

TO THE STUDENT

This book offers you a way to review selectively the principles of written English. Its programmed form of presentation enables you to learn efficiently with or without the direct supervision of an instructor.

The design of the text arises from the particular needs of advanced students who have studied grammar and usage in elementary and high schools. If you have had such training, you probably do not need another exhaustive course in English. Yet writing clear and effective prose for college courses and for a profession normally requires some additional study. This book accordingly provides a system which permits you to identify your individual deficiencies; in this way you can study as much or as little as you need, concentrating on those problems with which you have difficulty.

Since this is a programmed text, you should acquaint yourself with its organization before you begin to study.

First, glance through the book briefly. Notice that it is divided into individual paragraphs called *frames*. Notice also that certain frames, called *express frames*, are set apart in boxes. Each frame calls for one or more responses; the correct responses are in the margin beside the frames. As you will see, a blank space may represent one missing word, or it may represent several missing words. In many frames, you need only indicate a choice between two alternative responses.

The express frames—those set off in boxes—are at the beginning of each short sequence of frames dealing with a particular subject. When you begin to study, cover the answer column with an envelope or a folded piece of paper and read the first express frame. If you can complete it without difficulty, skip over the intervening frames to the next express frame. Your ability to complete an express frame indicates that you do not need to study the frames of the sequence that directly follows it.

Be sure to use wisely your option of skipping sequences. When completing an express frame, do not guess. Be sure you have a reason for your response. Any difficulty you encounter in completing an express frame is simply a signal that you need to study the following sequence of frames.

Be sure also to complete all the short review sequences. These are identified in the same way that the express frames are, by a box. If you do poorly on a review sequence, go over the preceding frames and identify the source of your difficulty before you proceed.

Students who used earlier versions of this text discovered that they studied most efficiently during short periods—twenty minutes to a half-hour long. Therefore, you will probably find that you will get the most from this text if your own study periods are relatively short.

Here in brief are your guides for using this text.

1. *Complete all the express frames in order.*
2. *If you have any difficulty with an express frame, skip it and complete the frames of the sequence which directly follows.*
3. *Complete all the short review sequences.*
4. *Repeat a section if you have difficulty with a review sequence.*
5. *Keep your study periods brief.*

James A. Gowen

ENGLISH REVIEW MANUAL

A PROGRAM FOR SELF-INSTRUCTION

□   *Several tall, husky troopers.*

does not
is not

This word group (does, does not) have a predicate. Therefore, it (is, is not) a clause.

cannot

□ Because the word group *Several tall, husky troopers* is not a clause, it (can, cannot) stand alone as a sentence.

□   *The colt frisking in the pasture.*

is not

This word group is not a clause because it lacks a predicate; therefore, it (is, is not) a sentence.

□   *The colt frisking in the pasture was born just last week.*

is   does

This group of words (is, is not) a clause because it (does, does not) have both a subject and a predicate.

□ Remember, then, that a clause is a group of words containing both a subject and a predicate. Any group of related words which lacks either a subject or a predicate is called a *phrase.*

The colt frisking in the pasture.

does not

This group of words (does, does not) have both a subject and a predicate.

phrase
cannot

□ Because the word group *The colt frisking in the pasture* does not have a predicate, it is a (clause, phrase) and therefore (can, cannot) stand alone as a sentence.

□   *The last of the reports.*

phrase
is not

This word group is a (clause, phrase) and therefore (is, is not) a sentence.

□   *The painting was sold quickly.*

clause
does

This group of words is a (clause, phrase) because it (does, does not) have both a subject and a predicate.

5

Some of the following word groups are clauses; some of them are phrases or strings of phrases. Mark the phrases P and the clauses Cl.

Cl ☐ *She forgot her hat and sunglasses.*

P ☐ *At the beach.*

P ☐ *Walking along a dirt road.*

P ☐ *Without turning around to face the audience.*

P ☐ *The construction crew working on the power lines.*

Cl ☐ *The construction crew is working on the power lines.*

Cl ☐ *The students gathered in a group.*

P ☐ *By the water fountain.*

P ☐ *The students standing in a group by the water fountain.*

P ☐ *Washing dishes, folding towels, ironing clothes, and then baking bread and cookies for the bake sale on Sunday.*

UNIT 3 SENTENCE COMPLETENESS: INDEPENDENT AND DEPENDENT CLAUSES

Unless you give me the money beforehand.

dependent
cannot

This clause is a(n) (independent, dependent) clause; it (can, cannot) stand alone as a sentence.

CHAPTER I

SENTENCE BOUNDARIES

	UNIT 1 RECOGNIZING SUBJECTS AND PREDICATES
fog/disappeared	Draw a slash between the complete subject and the complete predicate in the following sentence. *Almost all the low, dense fog disappeared within two hours after sunrise.*
Wood	☐ The sentence is the basic unit of expression. *Wood burns.* This sentence expresses something about (*Wood, burns*). ☐ The subject of a sentence names who or what the sentence is about. *Wood burns.*
subject	*Wood* is the _____ of this sentence.

□   *Gold melts.*

Gold

The subject of this sentence is (*Gold, melts*).

□ The predicate of a sentence expresses something about the subject.

   Gold melts.

predicate

Melts, then, is the (subject, predicate) of this sentence.

□ All sentences have two parts: the naming part, called the

subject
predicate

(subject, predicate), and the expressing part, called the (subject, predicate).

□ Most of the sentences we use have subjects and predicates made up of more than one word.

   Wood burns.
   Soft wood such as pine or spruce burns very rapidly.

Soft wood such
as pine or spruce

In the second sentence, the subject includes *wood* and all the words related to *wood*. Underline them.

□   *Gold melts*
   The gold in ore melts almost instantly in the smelting furnace.

melts almost instantly
in the smelting
furnace

In the second sentence, the predicate includes *melts* and all the words related to it. Underline them.

□ The term *complete subject* is used to label all the words in the subject. Similarly, all the words in the predicate are called the *complete predicate*. Here, to keep our terms simple, we will refer to the two parts of the sentence as the *subject* and the *predicate*.

   The neighborhoods in the northern part of the city grew much more slowly after 1960.

city/grew

Draw a slash (/) between the subject and the predicate of this sentence.

2

☐ Draw a slash between the subject and the predicate of each of the following sentences.

days/survived

> Almost all of the fourteen miners trapped underground for three days survived the grueling experience without injury.

building/carries

> The bookstore in the student union building carries all of the paperback books used in the history courses.

☐ Here is a very long sentence. Like the simplest sentence we've looked at, it has two parts—the subject and the predicate. Draw a slash between the subject and the predicate.

centuries/reveal

> The political changes in Mexico during the nineteenth and twentieth centuries reveal the country's growth from a disturbed and divided nation into one unified and relatively peaceful.

REVIEW

Draw a slash between the subject and the predicate of each of the following sentences.

mind/begins

☐ The development of the human mind begins at birth and continues throughout adulthood.

Basketball/is

☐ Basketball is a game of concentration, skill, and competition.

addiction/is

☐ One way of dealing with drug abuse and addiction is through drug rehabilitation programs.

Cobras/manufacture

☐ Cobras manufacture a type of poison known as neurotoxic.

size/was

☐ Coming from high school to a university this size was a tremendous shock for me.

high school/are

☐ Classes in high school are quite different from classes in college.

3

A course in medieval philosophy.

The only class meeting on Tuesdays and Thursdays is a course in medieval philosophy.

| phrase clause second | The first group of words is a (phrase, clause), and the second group is a (phrase, clause). Only one of the two word groups is a sentence, the (first, second). |

☐ A group of words is not a sentence unless it has a subject and a predicate.

> *Men work.*
> *All of the men in the construction crew.*

first

Only one of these word groups is a sentence, the (first, second).

☐ All of the men in the construction crew is not a sentence because it lacks a predicate.

> *All of the men in the construction crew working on the power lines.*
> *All of the men in the construction crew drew overtime this week.*

second

Only one of these word groups is a sentence, the (first, second).

☐ In the previous frame, *All of the men in the construction crew working on the power lines* is not a sentence because it lacks a (subject, predicate).

predicate

☐ A group of words having both a subject and a predicate is called a *clause*. Because a sentence must have both a subject and a predicate, a sentence (does, does not) have at least one clause.

does

4

☐ Some word groups have a subject and a predicate but are parts of other sentences.

> *He can come tomorrow.*
> *If he can come tomorrow.*

second

Both of these word groups have a subject (*he*) and a predicate (*can come tomorrow*). We can tell, however, that one of them, the (first, second), is part of another sentence that is not shown.

second

☐ When a clause is part of another sentence and not a separate sentence in its own right, it is called a *dependent clause*. In the last frame, the (first, second) example is a dependent clause and unable to stand alone as a sentence.

second

☐ Clauses which can stand alone as sentences are called *independent clauses*. Of the following examples, the (first, second) is an independent clause.

> *Although the bushes have been well cared for.*
> *The bushes have been well cared for.*

dependent

☐ *Although the bushes have been well cared for* is a(n) (dependent, independent) clause.

cannot

☐ A dependent clause (can, cannot) stand alone as a sentence.

☐ *Before the game is played on Saturday.*

is not
dependent

This word group is a clause because it has a subject (*game*) and a predicate (*is played on Saturday*). It (is, is not) a sentence because it is a(n) (dependent, independent) clause.

☐ *Because he promised to meet us at the dance.*

dependent
is not

This word group is a(n) (dependent, independent) clause. It (is, is not) a sentence.

independent

☐ In order for a word group to stand alone as a sentence, then, it must be a(n) (dependent, independent) clause.

7

Each of the following sentences has two clauses, one independent and the other dependent. Put a slash between the two clauses and underline the dependent clause.

tomorrow/<u>if the weather is nice.</u>

☐ I will leave tomorrow if the weather is nice.

class/<u>even though I usually oversleep.</u>

☐ I always make it to class even though I usually oversleep.

know/<u>that everyone was all right in spite of the storm.</u>

☐ I had to let them know that everyone was all right in spite of the storm.

child/<u>who didn't win a prize at the party.</u>

☐ Marty was the only child who didn't win a prize at the party.

know/<u>when the test results will be posted?</u>

☐ Do you know when the test results will be posted?

<u>When he called last night,</u>/he

☐ When he called last night, he asked me for the tickets to the concert.

<u>Although she always seems to be frowning,</u>/Linda

☐ Although she always seems to be frowning, Linda is actually very pleasant.

UNIT 4   DEPENDENT CLAUSES: SUBORDINATING CONJUNCTIONS AND SUBORDINATE CLAUSES

(Before) the alumni made their bequest

Before the alumni made their bequest, the library had fewer than a thousand books.

Underline the subordinate clause in the sentence above and circle the subordinating conjunction.

8

□ Dependent clauses normally begin with an introductory word.

> *He came.*
> *When he came, we left.*

(When)

The first sentence here is a dependent clause in the second sentence. Circle the introductory word.

□ The introductory word serves to join the dependent clause to the independent clause, even if the dependent clause comes first in a sentence.

Because
because

> *Because we left first, we got to the restaurant early.*
> *We got to the restaurant early because we left first.*

In each of these two sentences, the dependent clause is *because we left first* and the independent clause is *we got to the restaurant early*. Underline the word that introduces the dependent clause in each sentence and joins it to the independent clause.

if

□   *I will leave tomorrow if the weather is nice.*

The first clause in this sentence is *I will leave tomorrow*; the second clause is *if the weather is nice*. Underline the word in the sentence that introduces the second clause and joins it to the first.

though

□   *I always make it to class though I usually oversleep.*

Underline the word that introduces the second clause and joins it to the first.

□   *I will leave tomorrow if the weather is nice.*

second

The (first, second) clause is a dependent clause and unable to stand alone as a sentence.

□   *When the president was ready, the reporters began the questioning.*

first

The dependent clause in this sentence is the (first, second).

□ A word that joins two clauses is called a *conjunction*. If the conjunction makes one clause dependent on another, it is called a *subordinating conjunction*.

> Alice is supposed to call us when her parents arrive. Professor Dobbs postponed the biology exam because we have tests in two other courses next week.

Put a slash between the two clauses in each of the above sentences, and underline the subordinating conjunction that joins the two clauses.

us/when
exam/because

□ A dependent clause which is introduced by a subordinating conjunction is called a *subordinate clause*. Underline the subordinate clause in the following sentence and circle the subordinating conjunction that introduces the subordinate clause.

> I don't know when I've had so much fun.

(when) I've had
so much fun.

□ As we have seen, the subordinate clause can come before the independent clause it is linked to.

> Although the trees have been well cared for, they don't seem to be flourishing.

Underline the subordinate clause in the sentence above and circle the subordinating conjunction that introduces it.

(Although) the trees
have been well cared
for

□ Underline the subordinate clause in each of the following sentences and circle the subordinating conjunction that introduces it and links it to the independent clause.

> Since he wasn't there on time, we started without him.

> I've asked my roommate to hand in my paper for me because I won't be here tomorrow.

(Since) he wasn't
there on time
(because) I won't be
here tomorrow.

Underline the subordinate clause in each sentence and circle the subordinating conjunction.

(if) I have time.

☐ I will finish the work if I have time.

(because) he was ill.

☐ Bob went home because he was ill.

(until) she left.

☐ He waited until she left.

(after) he runs a few errands for me.

☐ Tom will finish his math homework after he runs a few errands for me.

(Unless) you are willing to practice

☐ Unless you are willing to practice, you will never learn to write well.

(Because) their differences were so great

☐ Because their differences were so great, the managers were unable to reach an agreement.

(Whenever) I come home late

☐ Whenever I come home late, my father is standing at the door waiting for me.

UNIT 5   DEPENDENT CLAUSES: RELATIVES AND RELATIVE CLAUSES

whose

whose name I mentioned

The man whose name I mentioned is his uncle.

In this sentence the relative _____ introduces the relative clause _____.

☐ Remember that dependent clauses normally begin with an introductory word.

(that)

He had found the dog in the park.
He brought home the dog that he had found in the park.

The first sentence here becomes a dependent clause in the second sentence. Circle the word that introduces the dependent clause.

☐ Normally, an introductory word joins the dependent clause to the independent clause. Circle the introductory word that joins the dependent clause to the independent clause in this sentence.

Where is that girl who used to room with Marie?

(who)

☐ There is a small class of words called *relative pronouns*—or just *relatives*. This group includes *that, which* and the forms of *who* (*who, whom, whose*). A dependent clause introduced by a relative is called a *relative clause*. Underline the relative clause in the following sentence and circle the relative that introduces it.

This is the problem that gave me the most trouble.

(that) gave me the
most trouble.

☐   *This is the problem that gave me the most trouble.*

The dependent clause in this sentence is *that gave me the most trouble.* The word *that* which introduces the dependent clause is a (subordinating conjunction, relative); therefore, the dependent clause in this sentence is a (subordinate clause, relative clause).

relative

relative clause

☐ Circle the relative in each sentence below and underline the relative clause.

The teacher collected the assignment sheets from the students who had finished.
This is the book which I requested.

(who) had finished
(which) I requested

☐ Often a relative clause interrupts a main clause. When this happens, the main clause is continued after the relative clause. Underline the relative clause in this sentence.

The teacher whose book I borrowed is Mr. Finley.

whose book I
borrowed

☐ *Hank indicated the man whose place I should take.*
The teacher asked the ones who had finished to keep quiet.

second

The relative clause in the (first, second) sentence interrupts the main clause.

☐ Underline the relative clause in each sentence.

that has a fur collar
who looked hopelessly
lost

The girl with the coat that has a fur collar is my sister.
The child, who looked hopelessly lost, stood on the corner and wept.

REVIEW

Underline the relative clause in each sentence and circle the relative that introduces it.

(that) *led to Camelot.*

☐ *He directed me to the road that led to Camelot.*

(who) *retired last*
year

☐ *Four history professors who retired last year collaborated in the preparation of this series of pamphlets and films.*

(that) *she gave*

☐ *The reasons that she gave were silly.*

(which) *had become*
too small for our
growing community.

☐ *A new wing was added to the hospital, which had become too small for our growing community.*

(whose) *position had*
been made obsolete
by the new computer

☐ *Mr. Taylor, whose position had been made obsolete by the new computer, was forced to retire early.*

Leave the books on the desk.

Identify the complete subject and the complete predicate in the sentence above.

(You)
Leave the books on the desk.

Subject _____.
Predicate _____.

☐ Remember that a sentence must have both a subject and a predicate.

I will close the windows.

subject
predicate

In this sentence the (subject, predicate) is *I,* and the (subject, predicate) is *will close the windows.*

☐ When the sentence has the subject *you,* it is sometimes written in the command form with the subject understood rather than explicitly stated.

You close the windows.
Close the windows.

The implied (understood) subject of the second sentence

(You)

is _____.

☐   *Close the windows.*

If the subject of this sentence is understood to be *you,* then the predicate of the sentence is _____

Close the windows.

_____.

☐   *Give me the dog's leash.*

You
Give me the dog's leash.

The implied subject of this sentence is _____;
the predicate of the sentence is

_____.

14

□ The command form may be used to give commands or orders, to make requests, and to give instructions.

Insert tab "A" in slot "B."
Go by way of Chicago.
Please pass the salt.

The subject of each of these sentences is understood to be

You

_____.

□   *Go by way of Chicago.*

Go by way of Chicago.

If the implied subject of this sentence is *you*, then the predicate of the sentence is

_____.

Don't go yet.

□   *Don't go yet.*

Underline the predicate of this sentence.

□ Notice that, although the command form does not have an explicit (stated) subject, it does have an implied (understood) subject. Since it has both a subject and a

is

predicate, a command with the implied subject *you* (is, is not) a complete sentence.

REVIEW

Write the implied subject in parentheses beside each command, and then underline the complete predicate.

(You) *Get here right away.*

□   *Get here right away.*

(You) *Don't call my house after 9:00.*

□   *Don't call my house after 9:00.*

(You) *Try to finish your lab report by yourself.*

□   *Try to finish your lab report by yourself.*

15

In each of the following sentences, only the independent clause has an implied subject; the dependent clauses have stated subjects. Underline the clause in each sentence that is in the command form with the implied subject *You*.

Come over

☐ *Come over after you finish dinner.*

Stand up

☐ *Stand up when the judge enters the courtroom.*

please close the windows and lock the cabinets and drawers.

☐ *Before you leave the office, please close the windows and lock the cabinets and drawers.*

UNIT 7   REVERSED SUBJECT-PREDICATE ORDER

several problems
Here are

Here are several problems.

The subject of this sentence is _____.
The predicate is _____.

☐ In English, the subject usually comes before the predicate.

The rain came down.

subject
predicate

The (subject, predicate) *The rain* comes before the (subject, predicate) *came down.*

☐ The normal subject-predicate order of the English sentence is sometimes reversed.

Down came the rain.

after

The subject of this sentence, *the rain,* comes (before, after) the predicate, *Down came.*

16

☐ We often use *here* or *there* to introduce the predicate of a sentence when the predicate comes before the subject.

> *Here comes Charlie.*
> *Charlie comes here.*

Although *Here* introduces the predicate of the first sentence, the subject of both sentences is _____.

Charlie

☐ Sentences in which the predicate is introduced by *here* or *there* are often reversible.

> *Here are three tacks.*
> *Three tacks are here.*

Reverse the order of the subject and predicate in this sentence:

> *Here is your lost book.*

_____

Your lost book is here.

☐ *There* introducing the predicate of a sentence is sometimes an empty word that we can drop if we reverse the order of the subject and predicate.

> *There are two cars in the garage.*
> *Two cars are in the garage.*

Reverse the order of the subject and predicate in this sentence, dropping *There* if it is not needed.

> *There were several heads of state at the meeting.*

_____

_____

Several heads of state were at the meeting.

☐ When they introduce a sentence, both *here* and *there* are part of the predicate, not part of the subject. Draw a line under the predicate of this sentence.

> *There is the lost child.*

<u>*There is*</u>

□ Draw a single line under the subject of this sentence and a double line under the predicate.

Here is the new edition of that book.

Here is the new edition of that book.

□ In sentences expressing a question, the predicate may be introduced by *when, where, how,* or *why.* If so, the subject may follow the predicate.

How are you?

The subject of this sentence is neither *How* nor *are* but

you

_____.

□ If *when, where, how,* or *why* introduces the predicate, it is part of the predicate.

Where is Herman?

Herman

Where is

The subject of this sentence is not *Where* but _____.

The predicate is _____.

□ Draw a single line under the subject of this sentence and a double line under the predicate.

How was the party?

How was the party?

□ No matter where it occurs in the sentence, then, the (subject, predicate) is the naming part of the sentence, and the (subject, predicate) is the expressing part of the sentence.

subject

predicate

REVIEW

Draw a single line under the subject of each sentence and a double line under the predicate.

There stood the opposing forces.

□ *There stood the opposing forces.*

Here are some application forms.

□ *Here are some application forms.*

Near the gate stood a large statue of the general on horseback.	☐ *Near the gate stood a large statue of the general on horseback.*
Where is your young friend?	☐ *Where is your young friend?*
Why did you leave?	☐ *Why did you leave?*
When is the next election?	☐ *When is the next election?*

UNIT 8   END PUNCTUATION

Add the punctuation necessary to complete the following quotations of the kind indicated.

(a) *St.''*	(a) [Statement] *"She lives at 1316 14th St"*
(b) *St.?''*	(b) [Question] *"Does she live at 1316 14th St"*
(c) *St.!''*	(c) [Exclamation] *"She lives at 1316 14th St"*

☐ We end our sentences with one of three punctuation marks: a period (.), a question mark (?), or an exclamation mark (!). A period marks the close of a statement. Punctuate this sentence.

fights.	*He went to the fights*

fights?	☐ *He went to the fights*

This sentence could be a question in certain circumstances. If it were, we would use a question mark. Punctuate it as a question.

fights!	☐ *He went to the fights*

In still different circumstances this sentence could be an exclamation—of the speaker's outrage, for instance. It would then require an exclamation mark. Punctuate it as an exclamation.

	☐ Normally, question and exclamation marks are used only at the ends of sentences. Periods, however, are used also to indicate abbreviation—Dr. (Doctor), Mr. (Mister), Ave. (Avenue). Punctuate this sentence.
Dr. Mrs. party.	*Dr and Mrs Bell will attend the party*
	☐ If an abbreviation comes at the end of a sentence requiring a period, one period will serve to indicate the abbreviation and to end the sentence:
St.	*He lives on Blair St*
	☐ If an abbreviation comes at the end of a sentence requiring a question mark or an exclamation mark, we must use a period to indicate the abbreviation. Complete the punctuation of this sentence.
St.?	*He lives on Blair St?*
	☐ Add the necessary punctuation to the following sentences.
St.?	(a) *Can you deliver this to the address on Main St*
St.	(b) *I already delivered it to that address on Main St*
	☐ *"What a wonderful party"* *"It was a wonderful party"*
the first	Normally, an exclamation mark will end (the first, both) sentence(s).
	☐ The normal use of an exclamation mark is to show that a speaker's voice is unusually loud. For instance, we punctuate a shout with an exclamation mark. Punctuate this shout.
Hey!	*Hey*
	☐ An exclamation mark is useful in direct quotations to indicate that a speaker has shouted or spoken loudly. Complete the punctuation of this sentence.
"Ouch!" he said.	*"Ouch" he said.*

□ In writing, we cannot shout at our readers. Forceful expression in prose is a matter of word choice and word order rather than voice level.

> *These are the times that try men's souls.*
> *Wow! These are really rough times!*

In spite of the exclamation marks, the second sentence (is, is not) as forceful as the first.

is not

□ The first sentence, written by Thomas Paine, is vigorous without an exclamation mark. The second sentence, by contrast, is feeble even though ended with an _____ mark.

exclamation

□ Just as shouting will not make an argument more convincing, ending a statement with an exclamation mark will not make it more vigorous. As a general rule, we should reserve the exclamation mark for direct quotation of shouted words or sentences.

> *"Look at that car"*
> *The car we saw was painted shocking pink*

Ordinarily we would end only the (first, second) sentence with an exclamation mark.

first

REVIEW

Add the necessary punctuation to the following sentences.

□ *Dr and Mrs Rogers will be out of town for the next few weeks*

Dr.   Mrs.
weeks.

□ *"Oh, no"*

no!"

□ *"Does he live on 10th St"*

St.?"

□ *"Look out"*

out!"

□ *My new address is 1015 Clarke St*

St.

The whole family accompanied Mike to the airport. To say goodbye and to let him know how sincerely they hoped for his safe return.

phrase
is not

The second group of words is a (clause, phrase); therefore, it (is, is not) a sentence.

☐ When we punctuate as a sentence a group of words that is not a complete sentence, the result is called a *fragment.*

Walking down the street yesterday. I ran into an old friend that I have not seen in years.

first

Of the examples above, the (first, second) is a fragment.

☐ Remember that a sentence must have both a subject and a predicate. A group of words which has a subject and a predicate is called a (clause, phrase).

clause

☐ Because a phrase is a word group without a subject and predicate, a phrase (can, cannot) stand alone as a sentence.

cannot

☐ Therefore, a phrase punctuated as a sentence (is, is not) a fragment.

is

☐   *He left his camera. At the beach.*

first
second

Of the word groups above, the (first, second) is a sentence; the (first, second) is a fragment.

☐   *Jones slipped and fell. Trying to reach the top shelf.*

first
second

Of the word groups above, the (first, second) is a sentence and the (first, second) is a fragment.

☐   *Pigs make poor pets. And worse roommates.*

sentence
fragment

The first group of words is a (sentence, fragment). The second group is a (sentence, fragment).

22

	☐ *By sending her a box of homemade chocolate chip cookies and fudge brownies.*
fragment phrase	This word group is a (sentence, fragment) because it is a (phrase, clause).

REVIEW

	Underline the phrase fragments in the following examples. If the example contains no phrase fragments, mark it C.
<u>Standing in the shadows</u> <u>by the door.</u>	☐ *I saw him quite clearly. Standing in the shadows by the door.*
<u>On the question of</u> <u>nuclear disarmament.</u>	☐ *The President was forthright in stating his position. On the question of nuclear disarmament.*
C	☐ *Nancy raced into the house, dropped her books on the desk, and then raced back out again without even stopping to let her mother know she had been home.*
<u>Sailing his boat on the</u> <u>beautiful lake near his</u> <u>summer cabin.</u>	☐ *He had several outdoor activities, but everyone knew which was his favorite. Sailing his boat on the beautiful lake near his summer cabin.*
	After the speech one person stood and asked a question. Which was obviously gauged to embarrass the speaker.
second cannot	The (first, second) word group is a dependent clause. A dependent clause (can, cannot) stand alone as a sentence.
dependent	☐ We have seen that a sentence must contain at least one clause—that is, it must have a subject and a predicate. However, we have also seen that some clauses are parts of other sentences and unable to stand alone as sentences in their own right. A clause which cannot stand alone as a sentence is a(n) (independent, dependent) clause.

☐ Remember that there are two kinds of dependent clauses: (a) a clause introduced by a subordinating conjunction (<u>subordinate clause</u>) and (b) a clause introduced by a relative (<u>relative clause</u>).

> *I didn't read the article you gave me because I had too much homework to do.*
> *I had too much homework to do, which kept me busy all night.*

subordinate
relative

The first example contains a (subordinate, relative) clause. The second example contains a (subordinate, relative) clause.

☐ A dependent clause should not be punctuated as a sentence because it is a fragment.

> *I would be having the time of my life. If I were there.*

second
fragment

Of the clauses above, the (first, second) is a dependent clause. Therefore, it is a (sentence, fragment).

☐   *Here is the watch. That I bought yesterday.*

second
dependent

The (first, second) clause is a fragment because it is a(n) (independent, dependent) clause.

☐ Correct any subordinate clause fragment in the following examples by joining it to the sentence it belongs to.

> *The driver veered sharply when he saw the stalled truck ahead. He avoided a collision by inches.*
> *I'm sure I could have helped you with the project. If you had called me instead of just giving up.*

project if

☐ Underline the relative clause fragments in the following examples.

> *The man in the gray suit is Marcy's uncle. Who has flown all the way from Istanbul to attend her wedding.*

Who has flown all the
way from Istanbul to
attend her wedding.

Which is the
only prerequisite
for Psychology
400.

> *This semester I am enrolled in Psychology 351. Which is the only prerequisite for Psychology 400.*

Underline any dependent clause fragments in the following examples. If an example has none, mark it C.

Which was scarcely visible from the street.

□ Four old oak trees screened the house. *Which was scarcely visible from the street.*

C

□ We finally got around to fixing the back door, which has not closed properly since last summer.

Although they were dressed for a party.

□ The guests seemed to be in a rather dark mood. *Although they were dressed for a party.*

When you paint the living room.

□ Be sure to use masking tape to protect the windows. *When you paint the living room.*

Who was so absorbed in his game that he did not even notice.

□ The teacher beckoned impatiently to the little boy. *Who was so absorbed in his game that he did not even notice.*

25

CHAPTER II

COMPLEMENTS

<table>
<tr><td></td><td>

UNIT 1   DIRECT OBJECTS
</td></tr>
<tr><td>

first
radios
</td><td>

John makes radios.
John works rapidly.

Of these sentences, only the (first, second) has a direct object, _____.
</td></tr>
<tr><td>

subject
predicate
</td><td>

☐ In Chapter I we learned that all sentences have two basic parts: the naming part, called the (subject, predicate); and the expressing part, called the (subject, predicate).
</td></tr>
<tr><td>

Boys
play
</td><td>

☐   *Boys play.*

In this two-word sentence, the word _____ is the subject, and the word _____ is the predicate.
</td></tr>
</table>

☐ If a predicate has only one word, that word will be a verb.

> *Boys play.*

is

In this sentence, *play* (is, is not) a verb.

☐ We can easily identify verbs because they are the only kinds of words that have a different form to indicate past time. For instance, *play* has the form *played*; *finish*, another verb, also has a form to indicate past time,

finished

_____.

☐ Mark the verbs in the following list of words. Remember, only verbs have a form to indicate past time.

wash   *remember*
carry

| *wash* | *among* | *remember* |
| *but* | *bicycle* | *carry* |

☐ Although every predicate contains at least one verb, some verbs cannot complete the predicate.

> *Paul swam . . . .*
> *Paul made . . . .*

complete
incomplete

In the first example the predicate is (complete, incomplete); in the second it is (complete, incomplete).

☐   *Paul made cabinets.*

cabinets

In this sentence the word _____ completes the predicate.

☐ Words that complete the predicate belong to a group of sentence parts called *predicate complements*, or simply *complements*.

> *Paul made cabinets.*

complement

In this sentence, *cabinets* is a predicate complement, or simply a _____.

□ There are several types of complements. The complement which receives the direct effect of an action verb is called the *direct object*.

    Paul made cabinets.

direct

made

Cabinets, then, is a _____ object because it receives the direct effect of the action verb _____.

□   *He gave a party.*

party

The direct object of the verb *gave* is _____.

□   *The shortstop threw the ball.*

ball

The direct object in this sentence is _____.

□   *The minister spoke well.*
    The minister gave a fine sermon.

second

sermon

Only the (first, second) sentence has a direct object. The direct object is _____.

□   *The glass was shattered by the falling limb.*
    The falling limb shattered the glass.

second

glass

Only the (first, second) sentence has a direct object. The direct object is _____.

REVIEW

In the following sentences, draw a slash between the subject and predicate and then underline the direct object of the verb. If the sentence has no direct object, write *none*.

Bob/drove   <u>car</u>

□ *Bob drove the car all the way to Chicago.*

car/ran   none

□ *The car ran well all the way to Chicago.*

beard/held   <u>tape</u>

□ *A man with a beard held the tape.*

She/put   <u>leash</u>

□ *She put the leash on the dog.*

28

Nancy/washed <u>*dishes*</u>	☐ *Nancy washed the dishes right after dinner.*
students/wrote none	☐ *The students wrote rapidly.*
students/finished <u>*exams*</u>	☐ *The students finished their exams quickly.*

UNIT 2 INDIRECT OBJECTS

	They gave me a surprise party on my birthday. *I quieted the frightened child by singing to him.*
first me	Of these sentences only the (first, second) has an indirect object. The indirect object is _____.

☐ A sentence which has a direct object may also have an additional complement as part of its basic structure.

> *The shortstop threw the ball.*
> *The shortstop threw John the ball.*

threw
ball

The second sentence has an additional complement, the word *John*, between the verb _____ and the direct object _____.

☐ A complement which appears between the verb and the direct object is called an *indirect object* because it receives the indirect effect of an action verb.

> *Helen made her friends a cake.*

cake
friends

In this sentence the direct object is _____. The indirect object is _____.

☐   *He handed Cathy the newspaper.*

Cathy

The indirect object in this sentence is _____.

verb
direct

☐ The indirect object always appears between the _____ and the _____ object.

☐ An indirect object characteristically expresses *to* or *for whom* something is done. Thus, the sentence *Helen made her friends a cake* can be expressed in another way: *Helen made a cake* _____ *her friends.*

for

☐   *The paymaster issued us the checks.*

Using the *to-or-for* device shows us that this sentence can be expressed in the following way: *The paymaster issued*

the checks to us

_____.

☐ Remember, however, that the indirect object always comes between the verb and the direct object. Therefore, if the sentence is rewritten using *to* or *for,* it does not have an indirect object any longer.

    Nelson wrote the Major a letter.
    Nelson wrote a letter to the Major.

first

Only the (first, second) sentence uses *Major* as an indirect object.

☐ The *to-or-for* device, then, can be used to identify the indirect object in a sentence or to give an alternative way of expressing the same sentence. Using this device, test the sentences below to find out which one has an indirect object.

    He called me a taxi.
    He called me a liar.

first

Only the (first, second) has an indirect object.

☐   *He called me a taxi.*
    He called me a liar.

Although we can say *He called a taxi for me,* we would not say *He called a liar for me.* This simple test, then, proves to us that the sentence *He called me a liar* (does, does not) have an indirect object.

does not

30

Use the *to*-or-*for* device to identify the indirect objects in the following sentences. If a sentence has an indirect object, underline it; if it does not have an indirect object, write *none*.

him

☐ *I gave him my book.*

editor

☐ *The columnist sent the editor a blistering reply.*

☐ *The editor sent the columnist to cover the local quilting bee.*

☐ *We hit the enemy with all the firepower we could muster.*

you

☐ *He wasn't doing you any favors.*

UNIT 3   SUBJECTIVE COMPLEMENTS

Earl became president.
Earl saw the president.

first

The verb in the (first, second) sentence is a state-of-being verb.

☐ There are two main sentence types in English:

    (a) Someone or something *does* something.
    (b) Someone or something *is* or *seems to be* something.

The verb in the first sentence type is commonly called an *action* verb, while the verb in the second sentence type is called a *state-of-being* verb.

I am unusually tired today.
I work far too late most nights.

first

second

The (first, second) sentence has a state-of-being verb which expresses what the subject is or seems to be; the (first, second) sentence has an action verb which expresses what the subject does.

31

☐ As long as a verb expresses something that the subject *does*, it is an action verb, even if the action is mental or abstract.

> *I thought so.*
> *Aunt Rose hoped fervently for a call from her brother.*

does

action

In each sentence the verb (does, does not) describe something that the subject does. Therefore, the verb in each sentence is a(n) (action, state-of-being) verb.

☐ Of the state-of-being verbs, the most common are the forms of the verb *to be*.

> *Mrs. Hendricks was the only person there.*
> *The dictionary is on the third shelf.*

state-of-being

In each of these sentences, the verb is a form of the verb *to be*. Therefore, each one is a(n) (action, state-of-being) verb.

☐ Remember that a state-of-being verb expresses what a subject is or seems to be rather than what a subject does. Besides the forms of the verb to be, there are several other verbs which can function as state-of-being verbs.

> *She seemed much older than her sister.*
> *I've felt sick all day.*

state-of-being

Since it expresses how the subject is or seems to be, the verb in each of these sentences is a(n) (action, state-of-being) verb.

☐ Notice that the same verb can function as a state-of-being verb in one sentence and an action verb in a different sentence.

> *I've felt sick all day.*
> *The doctor felt the sick child's forehead.*

first
second

In the (first, second) sentence the verb *felt* is a state-of-being verb; in the (first, second) sentence it is an action verb.

	☐ *You look pleased.* *Please look at these reports.*
state-of-being action	In the first sentence *look* is a(n) (action, state-of-being) verb; in the second sentence it is a(n) (action, state-of-being) verb.
	☐ *The ghost appeared suddenly.* *The child appeared less frightened than her father.*
action state-of-being	In the first sentence *appeared* is a(n) (action, state-of-being) verb; in the second sentence it is a(n) (action, state-of-being) verb.

REVIEW

	Identify the underlined verbs as either action verbs or state-of-being verbs.
posed—action *were*—state-of-being	☐ *The cat posed quietly beside the fire and cleaned its paws until they were immaculate.*
seems—state-of-being *was*—state-of-being	☐ *Sharon seems less depressed now than she was last week.*
be—state-of-being	☐ *Where will you be next summer?*
looks—state-of-being	☐ *The situation looks promising.*
direct object subjective complement	*They elected me.* *I was president for the rest of the year.* In the first sentence the complement is *me*, a _____ _____. In the second sentence the complement is *president*, a _____.

☐ Earlier in this chapter we saw that many action verbs require complements—that is, they need something to complete them. Like some action verbs, state-of-being verbs also require complements.

> *Terry is . . . .*
> *He seems . . . .*

do

The verbs in these sentences (do, do not) require something to complete them.

☐   *Terry is only a child.*

The complement in a sentence with a state-of-being verb always refers to the subject of the sentence. For this reason we call such complements subjective complements. Since it refers to the subject *Terry*, the noun *child* in this

is

sentence (is, is not) a subjective complement.

☐ When a state-of-being verb is followed by a subjective complement, it serves to link the subject to the subjective complement. For this reason, a state-of-being verb is called a *linking* verb.

> *Mark is captain of the team.*

In this sentence the verb *is* links the subject *Mark* with

is

the subjective complement *captain*. Therefore, *is* (is, is not) a linking verb.

☐   *He appears satisfied with the arrangement.*

appears
satisfied

In this sentence the linking verb _____ links the subject *He* to the subjective complement _____.

□ We can easily avoid confusing subjective complements with other kinds of complements. Just remember that a subjective complement occurs only after a linking (state-of-being) verb. The other complements (direct objects and indirect objects) occur only after action verbs.

> *I've felt sick all day.*
> *The doctor felt the sick child's forehead.*

linking
can
action
cannot

The first sentence has a(n) (action, linking) verb; therefore, it (can, cannot) have a subjective complement. The second sentence has a(n) (action, linking) verb; therefore, it (can, cannot) have a subjective complement.

REVIEW

Identify each underlined verb as either an action verb or a linking verb; then tell whether its complement is a direct object (DO) or a subjective complement (SC).

was—linking verb
champion—SC

□ *He was the champion.*

shattered—action verb
vase—DO

□ *One careless movement shattered the priceless vase.*

is—linking verb
one—SC

□ *Paula is the only one of my college friends I still write to.*

was—linking verb
person—SC
borrowed—action verb
notes—DO

□ *I don't know who was the last person who borrowed my notes.*

CHAPTER III

COORDINATION AND SUBORDINATION

UNIT 1   FORMING COMPOUND SENTENCES

The huge jet rolled to a stop. The dignitaries descended into a mob of waiting reporters.
The reporters had been waiting since midnight. General de Gaulle was due to arrive from Paris.

Decide which group of sentences would make a good compound sentence. Using the appropriate coordinating conjunction, join the sentences in a compound sentence.

_____

_____

_____

The huge jet rolled to a stop, and the dignitaries descended into a mob of waiting reporters.

☐ Occasionally we need to join two or more independent clauses—or sentences—into one sentence.

> *The packages arrived on time; the letters were late.*
> *Although the packages arrived on time, the letters were late.*

Only one of these sentences is composed of two independent clauses, the (first, second).

first

☐ We can join two or more independent clauses with a semicolon (;) or with a comma plus one of the seven words called coordinating conjunctions: *and, but, or, nor, for, so,* and *yet.*

> *The packages arrived on time, but the letters were late.*

Here two independent clauses are joined with the

_____ *but.*

coordinating conjunction

☐ Two or more independent clauses joined with a semicolon or a comma plus a coordinating conjunction is called a compound sentence.

> *The packages arrived on time, but the letters were late.*

This, then, is a _____.

compound sentence

☐
> *The living room was crowded, but the dining room was almost empty.*
> *The living room was crowded; the dining room was almost empty.*

Which of these sentences is or are compound, only the first or both?

both

☐ Joining closely related sentences into a compound sentence helps to stress their relationship.

> *I liked her. She liked me.*
> *I liked her, and she liked me.*

The relationship between the consecutive ideas is stressed in the (first, second) example.

second

□ Join the following closely related sentences in a compound sentence.

and the leaves
began to fall

> *The weather cooled. The leaves began to fall.*
> *The weather cooled,* _____
>
> _____ .

□ Form a compound sentence from the following sentences, using the appropriate coordinating conjunction.

but my right eye
requires correction

> *My left eye is perfect. My right eye requires correction.*
> *My left eye is perfect,* _____
>
> _____ .

□ Use the appropriate coordinating conjunction in the following compound sentences.

but
and

> *Hank agreed to help,* _____ *John refused.*
> *The chairman took the vote,* _____ *the resolution passed.*

□ Sentences should be combined in a compound sentence only if they are closely related.

> *The waves were choppy. The wind was cold.*
> *The waves were choppy. Lights flickered on the moored boats.*

first

Only the (first, second) group of sentences would make a good compound sentence.

□

> *The house is on a large lot. Its rooms are spacious.*
> *The house is on a large lot. The school is nearby.*

first

Only the (first, second) group of sentences would make a good compound sentence.

38

□ *The abandoned car had a smashed fender. Two of its tires were flat.*
The abandoned car had a smashed fender. The police towed it away.

Form a compound sentence from the one group of sentences that is closely related.

The abandoned car had _____
_____.

*a smashed fender, **and**
two of its tires were flat
or
a smashed fender; two
of its tires were flat*

REVIEW

Make a compound sentence of each of the following sentence groups that is closely related. Indicate which group or groups would not make a good compound sentence.

□ *Judy will be fifteen in August. Hank will be eighteen in November.*

_____
_____.

*August, **and** Hank
or
August; Hank*

□ *I was quite anxious to become a member of the committee. The board refused to accept my candidacy.*

_____
_____

*committee, **but***

□ *These lights were left on all day. Tomorrow, make sure that they are turned off promptly at 8 A.M.*

_____
_____

This group would
not make a good
compound sentence.

Correct the punctuation in these sentences if necessary.
Mark correct sentences C.

(a) *skillet; she*
or
skillet. She
(b) C

   (a) *He grabbed the skillet she grabbed the coffeepot.*
   (b) *He grabbed the skillet just as she grabbed the cof-
      feepot.*

□ We punctuate all independent clauses separately as sentences unless they are parts of a compound sentence.

The water was cold, but we went in swimming anyway.

is

does

This (is, is not) a compound sentence because it (does,
does not) have two independent clauses.

□ We can separate the independent clauses of a compound
sentence with a comma plus a coordinating conjunction
(*and, but, or, nor, for, so,* and *yet*), or we can separate
them with a semicolon.

*She forgot her appointment last week, and she was late
for work twice this week.*

and

The parts of this compound sentence are joined by a
comma plus the coordinating conjunction _____.

□   *She forgot her appointment last week; she was late for
work twice this week.*

Here the parts of the compound sentence are joined by a

semicolon

_____.

40

□ Either a comma plus a coordinating conjunction or a semicolon should join parts of a compound sentence.

> *The TV repairman sent his bill the furniture store will send a bill later.*

are not · The parts of this compound sentence (are, are not) properly joined.

□ A compound sentence with its parts not separated by either a comma plus a coordinating conjunction or a semicolon is called a *fused sentence*.

> *The TV repairman sent his bill the furniture store will send a bill later.*

is · This (is, is not) an example of a fused sentence.

□ Correct this sentence without using a coordinating conjunction.

bill; the
> *The TV repairman sent his bill the furniture store will send a bill later.*

□ Now correct the same sentence using a coordinating conjunction.

bill, **and** the
> *The TV repairman sent his bill the furniture store will send a bill later.*

□ Add whatever is necessary to the following sentences.

college; nurses
or
college, and nurses
> *Doctors normally study for 6 years in college nurses study for at least 3 years.*

no additions
are necessary
> *Hang gliding is a recently developed sport, while sky diving developed much earlier.*

□ Fused sentences are hard to read because the place where one independent clause ends and another begins is not immediately clear. Add whatever is necessary to the following sentences.

10 percent; the
or
*10 percent, **and** the*

> *Tomorrow the prices of all appliances will be reduced by 10 percent the price of all radios will be reduced by 20 percent.*

time; try
or
*time, **and***

> *In the future, try to be ready on time try to remember to bring your money also.*

□ Remember that if we do not use a semicolon between parts of a compound sentence, we use a comma plus a coordinating conjunction.

> *Yesterday afternoon the families went to the beach, the day before they went to the zoo.*

is not

This sentence (is, is not) adequately marked.

□ A comma without a coordinating conjunction between parts of a compound sentence is called a *comma splice*.

> *Yesterday afternoon the families went to the beach, the day before they went to the zoo.*

comma splice

This sentence contains an example of a _____.

□ Sentences with comma splices are almost as confusing to read as fused sentences. Remember, if we don't use a semicolon between parts of a compound sentence, we need both a comma and a coordinating conjunction. Correct both of these sentences.

arrived; we
or
*arrived, **and***

> *The plane finally arrived, we were able to board immediately.*

dormitories; eight
or
*dormitories, **and***

> *Seven players were living in student dormitories eight others were living in apartments near campus.*

☐ Independent clauses in compound sentences are often joined by conjunctive adverbs: *therefore, however, moreover, nevertheless, consequently,* and the like.

I won't go today; moreover, I'll never go with him.

The relationship between the independent clauses in this sentence is expressed by the conjunctive adverb _____.

moreover

☐ Conjunctive adverbs are different from coordinating conjunctions. As its name indicates, a conjunctive adverb is a connective; but unlike a coordinating conjunction, it can appear in several positions within its clause.

The girl wouldn't tell me her name; nevertheless, she did / give me her phone number / .

Nevertheless (can, cannot) appear in the other positions marked by the slanted lines.

can

☐ A coordinating conjunction, however, cannot appear in other positions but only at the division between clauses.

The girl wouldn't give her name, but she did / give her phone number / .

The coordinating conjunction *but* (can, cannot) be moved to the positions marked by the slanted lines.

cannot

☐ A conjunctive adverb's mobility within its own clause distinguishes it from a coordinating conjunction. It belongs to one clause within a compound sentence, not both, and to show this function, we use a semicolon rather than a comma preceding it.

He was outraged; however, he calmed down later.

Substituting a comma for the semicolon in this sentence (is, is not) possible.

is not

☐ *And, but, or, for,* and *yet* are coordinating conjunctions. *However, moreover, nevertheless,* and *consequently* are conjunctive adverbs. Punctuate these sentences.

(a) *times; nevertheless,*

(a) *The motor stalled three times nevertheless, we were able to get home.*

(b) *repairs, but*

(b) *The motor was due for major repairs but we delayed them because of the expense.*

☐ If necessary, correct the punctuation in these sentences.

(a) *days; nevertheless,*

(a) *We invited him to stay for 3 days, nevertheless, he stayed for 8.*

(b) *We invited him to stay for 3 days, but he stayed for 8.*

☐ However, if we use a coordinating conjunction with a conjunctive adverb, a comma is adequate.

The weatherman predicted rain for Wednesday, and consequently the skies cleared by noon.

Since the conjunctive adverb *consequently* is preceded by the coordinating conjunction *and,* the comma in this sentence (should, should not) be changed to a semicolon.

should not

☐ Add the necessary punctuation to these sentences.

(a) *weeks, but*

(a) *I hadn't studied for 3 weeks but nevertheless I took the test.*

(b) *carefully; however*

(b) *The trees were planted carefully however, three of them failed to take root.*

☐ If clauses joined by a coordinating conjunction have other commas, it is a good practice to make the division between them with a semicolon rather than a comma.

If this paint remover works, I won't regret paying that much for it, but if it doesn't, I'll demand my money back.

It would be helpful to substitute a semicolon for the comma preceding _____.

but

□ A comma dividing clauses which have other commas is easily overlooked. A semicolon will help the reader find the division between the clauses more readily. Correct the punctuation in this sentence.

be late; and

> *Unless you're ready, we'll be late, and if we're one minute late, we won't get in the door.*

□ Correct the punctuation where necessary in these sentences.

(a) it; but

> (a) *If you recommend it, I'll buy it, but even so, I won't promise to like it.*
>
> (b) *Along the lakefront is a low range of hills, and behind that the Blue Ridge is distantly visible.*

REVIEW

night; the
or
*night, **and** the*

Add whatever is necessary to the following sentences. Mark correct sentences C.

□ *The lights were left on all night the doors were unlocked.*

ten; however

□ *John left the party at around ten, however, his wife remained until after midnight.*

C

□ *The children were unhappy with the babysitter because she made them sit outside.*

scaffolding; the
or
*scaffolding, **and** the*

□ *Two men in the construction crew are responsible for the scaffolding the remaining ten men are responsible for the large tools.*

floor; and

□ *When Helen came home, she threw her coat on the floor, and her mother, who had had a hard day, shouted at her to hang it in the closet.*

Correct the following sentences where necessary.

left and

> *The pilot banked the airplane steeply to the left; and started his descent toward O'Hare Airport.*

gates, although

> *All of the people trying to crowd into the rock concert were milling around the gates; although the concert was not to begin for four hours.*

☐ Remember that we can join closely related independent clauses with a semicolon.

> *The Sierra Nevada Mountains form the eastern boundary of California the Rocky Mountains form the western border of the Midwest.*

Here a semicolon should appear after the word _____ _____.

California

☐ An independent clause must come before and after a semicolon.

> *She can come; although she should really stay home today.*

incorrect
is not

Here the semicolon is (correct, incorrect) because what comes after it (is, is not) an independent clause.

☐ Inexperienced writers tend to use the semicolon mistakenly as an elegant substitute for a comma. In fact, the semicolon is more like a period, showing the division between independent clauses.

> *He left for the day before five trying to beat the rush-hour traffic.*

comma

Here we need a (comma, semicolon) after *five*.

☐ *The dogs began to bark and jump around the pen when they saw their owner bringing their food.*
The dogs began to bark and jump around the pen the cats came running out of the barn.

the second

A semicolon can follow *pen* in (the second, both) sentence(s).

☐ Fragments that result from the misuse of the semicolon create the same kind of reading difficulties as fragments that result from the misuse of the period. That is, readers expect an independent clause after both a period and a semicolon.

The senator waited patiently. Until the angry buzzing among the crowd subsided.
The senator waited patiently; until the angry buzzing among the crowd subsided.

both

Until begins a fragment in (the first, both) example(s).

☐ A phrase or a dependent clause joined to an independent clause with a semicolon is a fragment just as it would be if it were punctuated with a period.

The expensive pictures hung on the far wall; lighted by a series of bright floodlamps.

is

What follows the semicolon here (is, is not) a fragment.

☐ Avoid fragments that result from the misuse of the semicolon by making sure any semicolon you use joins independent clauses, not dependent clauses or other sentence parts.

The Christmas presents were all carefully wrapped in bright paper; and were arranged in stacks around the base of the tree.

is

The part after the semicolon here (is, is not) a fragment.

47

□ Put a semicolon where needed in these sentences.

top; the

> *The first car was red with a white vinyl top the second car was solid blue.*
>
> *The first car was red with a white vinyl top with a sticker price of $6050.*

□

> *All of the lights in the northern section of the city went out at 11 P.M.; power was not restored until 8 A.M. the next morning.*
>
> *We could see the rainbow to the east of us just below the clouds; arching from one mountain to the next.*

A fragment results from the misuse of the semicolon in

the second

(the second, both) sentence(s).

REVIEW

Mark with an X any of the following sentences having a fragment caused by the misuse of the semicolon. Mark correct sentences C.

C

□ *The TV worked perfectly all week; now, just as I turned it on, I could hardly get a picture.*

X

□ *The houses on the east side of the street were in serious disrepair; with peeling paint, broken windows, and cluttered porches.*

X

□ *Coffee prices have increased significantly over the past several years; causing many customers to choose alternate beverages such as tea and cereal drinks.*

X

□ *The president went on record as favoring the less controversial measure; thus inviting the hostility of the congressmen who had backed the other.*

48

*Four civilians were wounded during the rioting in Cara-
cas.*
Two soldiers were also wounded.

These sentences can be combined:

*and two soldiers were
wounded during the
rioting in Caracas*

Four civilians _____
_____
_____.

☐ We can often combine two sentences in one.

Harry went to a movie last night. Al went with him.
Harry and Al went to a movie last night.

The second, more economical expression of identical ideas

is

(is, is not) as clear as the first.

☐ Two successive sentences with different subjects but similar predicates can often be combined in one sentence
without loss of clarity.

The Ford is for sale. So is the Chevrolet.

The ideas expressed in these two sentences can easily be
combined in one sentence.

and the Chevrolet

The Ford _____ *are for sale.*

☐   *The Harrells live in Oceanside. The Randalls live in that
same city.*

These sentences can be combined in one sentence having
a compound subject.

and the Randalls

The Harrells _____ *live in Oceanside.*

☐ *These letters can be mailed today. That package can be mailed too.*

Combine these sentences in one.

These letters _____ _____.

and that package can be mailed today

☐ Two sentences with subjects that refer to the same person or thing and with different predicates can often be combined in one sentence with a compound predicate.

Perkins called room service. He ordered a club sandwich.

Combine these sentences in one.

Perkins called room service _____.

and ordered a club sandwich

☐ *This television set has the usual front tuning devices. It has an additional fine tuner in back.*

These sentences can be made into one having a compound direct object.

This television set has the usual front tuning devices _____.

and an additional fine tuner in back

REVIEW

Form a single sentence from each of the following sentence groups.

The Martins and the Caldwells visited us yesterday.

☐ *The Martins visited us yesterday. So did the Caldwells.*

_____
_____

The chemist added sulfuric acid carefully to the water and then poured the mixture into a large beaker.

☐ *The chemist added sulfuric acid carefully to the water. He then poured the mixture into a large beaker.*

_____
_____

The new humanities building and the law school will be built during the years 1983–1984.	☐ *The new humanities building will be constructed during the years 1983–1984. The law school will be built during those years also.* _____ _____

UNIT 5 PUNCTUATING COMPOUND SENTENCE PARTS

The comma following *carefully* should be omitted.	If necessary, correct the punctuation in this sentence. *Dr. Bronson examined Mr. Burns carefully, and afterwards recommended a long rest.*

and	☐ Coordinating conjunctions are used to join compound sentence elements as well as independent clauses in compound sentences. *She cut the vegetables and cooked the stew.* This is not a compound sentence but a sentence with a compound predicate. Its parts, *cut the vegetables* and *cooked the stew*, are joined by a coordinating conjunction, _____.
incorrect	☐ The division between two parts of a compound sentence element is usually not punctuated with a comma or a semicolon. *Both his backstroke and his crawl needed improvement.* A comma before *and* in this sentence would be (correct, incorrect) because it joins parts of a compound subject.
first	☐ Before placing a comma before *and*, we should make sure that it joins independent clauses in a compound sentence and not compound sentence elements. *He took his football and went home.* *He took his football and the team went home.* A comma before *and* would be incorrect in the (first, second) sentence because it joins the parts of a compound predicate.

□ Add any necessary punctuation to these sentences. Remember, we should not separate two compound sentence parts with a comma.

    (a) *We take Math 1 this semester and Geometry the next.*

(b) *Thursdays, and on Thursdays*

    (b) *Our gym class meets on Tuesdays and Thursdays and on Thursdays we swim.*

□ Add any necessary punctuation to these sentences.

    (a) *He felt that trying hard didn't pay off and simply quit.*

(b) *can, but*

    (b) *He thought he had tried as hard as a person can but he could have tried harder.*

REVIEW

Change or add punctuation where necessary in the following sentences. Mark sentences correctly punctuated C.

The comma after *oil* is incorrect.

□ *He added a friction-proofing compound to the oil, and made it a habit to change the oil every 1000 miles.*

C

□ *The painters failed to put a good undercoat on the board and painted directly over cracked and chipped paint.*

The comma after *passer* is incorrect.

□ *Roberts is, on the whole, a fine passer, and runs well on the option plays.*

UNIT 6 SUBORDINATE CLAUSES

Because I had a flat tire, I was late.
or
I was late because I had a flat tire.

Revise the following sentence, logically subordinating one of its ideas.

    I had a flat tire and I was late.

_____

☐ Although the coordinating conjunction *and* is useful in joining two or more closely related ideas, it is the most misused connective in our language.

> *We didn't water the lawn, and it dried up.*
> *The lawn dried up because we didn't water it.*

second

Of these two sentences, which express the same ideas, only the (first, second) adequately expresses the relationship between the ideas.

☐ *We didn't water the lawn, and it dried up.*
> *The lawn dried up because we didn't water it.*

because

Comparing these examples shows the weakness of the first. We should never use the coordinating conjunction *and* carelessly as a substitute for the subordinating conjunction _____.

☐ The relationship between ideas is often better expressed with a subordinating conjunction such as *because* than with a coordinating conjunction such as *and*.

> *The chair was weak, and the table had a broken top.*
> *The chair was weak and it collapsed.*

The relationship between the ideas in one of these sentences would be clearer if expressed with *because*:

it collapsed

> *Because the chair was weak,* _____.

☐ The grammatical effect of a subordinating conjunction on a clause it introduces is that it makes the clause a dependent—a subordinate—unit.

> *Because the chair was weak, it collapsed.*

because

In this sentence the subordinating conjunction _____ subordinates its clause to the main clause, *it collapsed*.

☐ Often the relationship between two or more ideas is clear only if one idea is subordinated.

> She behaved rudely, and Pete didn't ask her out again.

This sentence contains a clause requiring subordination:

because she behaved rudely

> Pete didn't ask her out again _____.

☐ Normally, a cause-and-effect relationship is clearer if the statement of the cause is subordinated to the statement of its effect. *Because* and *since* are the subordinating conjunctions we use for this.

> The workman failed to fasten his safety belt, and he fell.

Subordinate the idea of cause in this sentence, using *since*.

Since the workman failed to fasten his safety belt

> _____,
> he fell.

Since [Because] we made two calls to New Orleans, our phone bill was unusually high.

or

Our phone bill was unusually high because we made two calls to New Orleans.

☐ > We made two calls to New Orleans, and our phone bill was unusually high.

☐ Rewrite this sentence, logically subordinating one idea to the other.

> _____
> _____

☐ Rewrite the following sentence, logically subordinating one idea to the other.

Unless the painters finish within a week, I told him, we can't move in on time.

> Either the painters finish within a week, I told him, or we can't move in on time.
> _____
> _____

54

□ Two kinds of statements often linked together are a conditional statement and a statement of its consequences.

If he helps, we'll finish early.

The statement of the consequences, *we'll finish early,* is qualified by a conditional statement, _____.

If he helps

□ Making a conditional statement an independent clause in a compound sentence is often unsatisfactory.

You hit me, and I'll hit you.
If you hit me, I'll hit you.

These examples show that the relationship between the condition and its consequence is clearer if the condition is expressed as a subordinate clause introduced by

If

_____.

□ Normally, a condition should be subordinated to the consequence, using *if* or *unless.*

You get that bridge straightened, or you'll have trouble with the rest of your teeth.

Subordination will improve this sentence:

Unless you get that bridge straightened

_____,
you'll have trouble with the rest of your teeth.

□ *You work tonight, and I'll examine your progress later.*
You work tonight, and you'll be paid overtime.

The first part of one of these sentences is a condition that should be subordinated:

you'll be paid overtime

If you work tonight, _____.

□ *Either the Senate passes the bill by November, or the House of Representatives will not be able to discuss it this term.*

Unless the Senate passes the bill by November, the House of Representatives will not be able to discuss it this term.

Subordinate the idea of condition in this sentence.

_____
_____

55

□ Rewrite the following sentence, stressing by subordination the time relationship between the two events.

A child has to develop his leg muscles, and then he can learn to walk.

_____

_____

A child has to develop
his leg muscles before
he can learn to walk.

□ Using *and* to stitch together ideas which are related in time often produces sentences which are crudely inexact.

I was running for the bus, and he tried to stop me.
While I was running for the bus, he tried to stop me.

These examples show that the time relationship of the two events (is, is not) expressed more clearly in the second example.

is

□ The expression of two events related in time is usually clearer if one event is expressed as a subordinate clause.

He had finished his work, and he called me.

This sentence will be clearer if the first event is expressed in a subordinate clause.

he had finished
his work

After _____, *he called me.*

□ English has a variety of subordinating conjunctions useful in expressing time relationships: *before, when, while, as, after, since,* and *until.* Normally we should use one of these to link our expressions of events related in time and thus avoid the clumsiness resulting from the use of *and.*

We waited, and the motor finally died.

Rewrite this sentence, using *until* as the subordinating conjunction.

until the motor
finally died

We waited _____.

☐   *The pilot learned that his fuel was low, and he tried to land immediately.*

Rewrite this sentence, using *when*.

When the pilot learned that his fuel was low, he tried to land immediately.

_____

_____

☐   *The car turned into the steep street, and it skidded.*

Rewrite this sentence, using *as*.

As the car turned into the steep street, it skidded.

_____

_____

☐   *The electrician found that he had to clean the wires, and then he could join them.*

Rewrite this sentence, subordinating the second part.

The electrician found that he had to clean the wires

before he could join them

_____.

☐ Rewrite these sentences as one, stressing by subordination Mr. Ellis' presidency.

Mr. Ellis is the president of our cooperative. He owns 4 acres of lemon trees.

Mr. Ellis, who owns 4 acres of lemon trees, is the president of our cooperative.

_____

_____

☐ The relatives *who, whose, whom, which,* and *that* are useful in combining closely related ideas which would be crudely expressed as independent clauses or sentences.

Charlie is my cousin. He lives with us.
Charlie, who lives with us, is my cousin.

The relationship between the ideas here is better expressed in the (first, second) example.

second

□   *Charlie is my cousin. He lives with us.*
     Charlie, who lives with us, is my cousin.

By substituting *who* for *He*, the second sentence in the first example becomes a relative _____ in the second example.

□   *The sewage plant cost $500,000. It serves Elk County.*

By substituting *which* for *It*, we can use the second sentence as a relative clause modifying *plant*:

     The sewage plant _____
     cost $500,000.

□   *Marge has an attractive brother. Liz dates him regularly.*

We can make the second sentence into a relative clause.

     Marge has an attractive brother whom _____
     _____.

□   *Lee Construction won the road improvement contract. It will soon be the largest firm of its kind in the state.*

The second sentence can serve as a relative clause in the first:

     Lee Construction, _____ the largest firm of its kind in the state, won the road improvement contract.

□   *Elliot McGill has become General Sales Manager. He had been the West Coast representative.*

Combine these sentences in one, making the second a relative clause.

     Elliot McGill, _____
     _____

□ When we subordinate with a relative clause, we should express the more important idea as the main clause, the less important as the relative clause.

The camping trailer which sleeps three costs $1200.
The camping trailer which costs $1200 sleeps three.

cost

size

The more important idea in the first sentence is the (cost, size) of the trailer. The more important idea in the second is its (cost, size).

□ *Burns worked here 3 years. He was fired yesterday.*

Join these sentences in one, stressing the firing.

who worked here 3 years, was fired yesterday

Burns, _____
_____.

□ *Burns worked here 3 years. He was fired yesterday.*

Now join these sentences in a way that stresses the length of employment.

who was fired yesterday, worked here 3 years

Burns, _____
_____.

□ *The medical building is ten stories tall. It has fifty offices.*

Join these sentences in a way that stresses the height of the building.

which has fifty offices, is ten stories tall

The medical building, _____
_____.

□ *Mack had worked with me in Hawaii. He visited us last week.*

Join these sentences in a way that stresses the visit.

who had worked with me in Hawaii, visited us last week

Mack, _____
_____.

Rewrite the following sentences, logically subordinating one idea to the other in each.

Unless you pay your bill by next Tuesday, we will turn the matter over to our lawyers.

☐ *Either you pay your bill by next Tuesday or we will turn the matter over to our lawyers.*

_____

_____

Because [Since] the tanks on gasoline trucks are vented, they cannot explode.

☐ *The tanks on gasoline trucks are vented, and they cannot explode.*

_____

_____

Ralph Jones, who worked for me last year, is now working in the engineering department.
or
Ralph Jones, who is now working in the engineering department, worked for me last year.

☐ *Ralph Jones worked for me last year; he is now working in the engineering department.*

_____

_____

Although [Though, While] Pete began mowing the lawn at 9 A.M., he is not finished yet.

☐ *Pete began mowing the lawn at 9 A.M., but he is not finished yet.*

_____

_____

UNIT 7 PUNCTUATING SUBORDINATE CLAUSES

Add any necessary punctuation to these sentences.

(a) *We cannot ship your order until the factory supplies us with the model you requested.*

(b) requested, we

(b) *Until the factory supplies us with the model you requested we cannot ship your order.*

□ As a general rule, subordinate clauses—those introduced by subordinating conjunctions such as *if, while,* and *until*—are not separated from the main clause by a comma if they follow the main clause.

> *I'll go when you go.*

A comma would be incorrect before *when* because the subordinate clause (precedes, follows) the main clause.

follows

□ If a subordinate clause comes before the main clause, we separate the two clauses with a comma. Punctuate this sentence.

go, I'll

> *When you go I'll go.*

□ Add a comma where needed.

(a) *repaired, we*

> (a) *Until the refrigerator is repaired we cannot store frozen foods.*
> (b) *We cannot store frozen foods until the refrigerator is repaired.*

□ Punctuate these sentences where necessary.

> (a) *You have a good memory if you can remember that.*
(b) *that, you* > (b) *If you can remember that you have a good memory.*

□ Many writers prefer not to use a comma to separate from the main clause a subordinate clause introducing a sentence if the separation between the clauses is clear without it.

> *Until the refrigerator is repaired, we cannot store frozen foods.*

Because the division between the introductory clause and the main clause is clear, the comma in this sentence (is, is not
is not) necessary.

☐ However, omitting the comma following an introductory clause may cause trouble.

> *While Tom was fighting Harry and Bob were running away.*

We have to read this sentence at least twice to make sense of it. A comma signaling the end of the introductory clause—that is, after the verb _____—will make misreading impossible.

fighting

☐ If you wish to omit the comma after introductory clauses, be sure that the omission will not cause a reader difficulty.

> *Until he had returned the package remained on the table.*
> *Until he called for it the package remained on the table.*

A comma following the introductory clause is optional in the (first, second) sentence. It is necessary in the (first, second) sentence.

second   first

☐ Add any comma necessary in the following sentences.

(a) *appointed, the*

(b) *discharged, the*

    (a) *When I am appointed the company representative will get my help.*
    (b) *When the gun discharged the remaining bullet struck the floor.*

☐ It is always possible that our reader will have to hunt for the end of an introductory clause. Perhaps the best practice is to use a comma at the end of all such clauses. Punctuate these sentences accordingly.

(a) *lies, we*

(b) *certain, some*

    (a) *If we forget where our duty lies we are faithless to ourselves.*
    (b) *Since we cannot always be certain some say we learn nothing.*

Change or add punctuation where necessary in the following sentences. Mark correct sentences C.

☐ *He found he could not relax even though he certainly tried hard.*

C

☐ *The advance mechanism of his camera jammed, because he had threaded the film improperly.*

The comma is
unnecessary.

permissive, the

☐ *Whereas the child's father was permissive the mother was overly strict.*

A comma after *left*
is optional.

☐ *When he left we felt a good deal better.*

UNIT 8 PUNCTUATING RESTRICTIVE AND NONRESTRICTIVE CLAUSES

Add any necessary punctuation to these sentences.

(a) *The jacket which I am wearing now was a gift from my mother.*

(b) *San Francisco,*
which   water, is

(b) *San Francisco which is surrounded on three sides by water is an important banking center.*

☐ The relationship between a relative clause and the noun it follows is often signaled by commas. If the clause is not essential in identifying the noun, it is set off with commas—that is, a comma appears at both ends of the clause.

Henry, who had a cold last week, is now well.

Since the clause *who had a cold last week* is not essential

commas

in identifying Henry, it is set off with _____.

63

□   *The student who had a cold last week is now well.*

In this sentence the relative clause *who had a cold last week* (is, is not) essential in identifying which student is referred to.

is

□ Relative clauses essential to identify the nouns they modify are called restrictive clauses. Those which are not, but which merely add information, are called nonrestrictive clauses.

> *Henry, who had a cold last week, is now well.*
> *The student who had a cold last week is now well.*

The relative clause *who had a cold last week* is restrictive in the (first, second) sentence and nonrestrictive in the (first, second) sentence.

second
first

□ Restrictive clauses are not set off with commas. Nonrestrictive clauses are set off with commas to show that the information they contain is additional rather than essential.

> *The boat which sank cost $800.*
> *The boat, which I cherished because of its price, sank yesterday.*

The adjective clause *which sank* is (restrictive, nonrestrictive); *which I cherished because of its price* is (restrictive, nonrestrictive).

restrictive

nonrestrictive

□ Add the necessary commas to these sentences. Remember that we use a comma both before and after a nonrestrictive clause.

(a) *Nevada, which*
    country, has

(a) *Nevada which attracts tourists from all over the country has a small permanent population.*
(b) *The California that I remember was a good deal different from the California of today.*

64

□ If a nonrestrictive clause comes at the end of a sentence, only one comma is necessary to set it off. Add any necessary comma to these sentences.

(a) *husband, who*

    (a) *She loves her husband who gambles more than a poor man should.*
    (b) *Beware of marrying a man who gambles more than he should.*

□ Many relative clauses are restrictive or nonrestrictive, depending on meaning.

> *The witness who was stubborn refused to discuss the matter.*
> *The witness, who was stubborn, refused to discuss the matter.*

restrictive

To identify one witness among several, *who was stubborn* is (restrictive, nonrestrictive) in the first sentence. To show that *who was stubborn* is simply additional information about the only witness, the clause is (restrictive,

nonrestrictive

nonrestrictive) in the second sentence.

□   *Students, who seldom read, cannot expect their education to mean much.*
    Students who seldom read cannot expect their education to mean much.

first

The punctuation of *who seldom read* in the (first, second) sentence indicates that no student reads much. The punc-

second

tuation of this same clause in the (first, second) sentence indicates only that some students do not read much.

□   *People, who ask too many questions, irritate me.*

all

The punctuation of this sentence suggests that (some, all) people ask too many questions.

☐ Be sure that your commas signal the meaning you intend.

I respect teachers who are tough-minded.

will not
will

If we want this sentence to refer to only some teachers, we (will, will not) add a comma before *who*. If we wish it to refer to all teachers, we (will, will not) add a comma before *who*.

REVIEW

Change or add punctuation where necessary in the following sentences. Mark correct sentences C.

Sterling, who
Greece, began

☐ *Charles Sterling who was with our tour group in Greece began graduate school this semester.*

Both commas should
be omitted.

☐ *All cars, which have cracked windshields, will not receive certification from the Department of Motor Vehicles until the windshields are replaced.*

C

·☐ *Members who become inactive forfeit their voting rights.*

jig, which

France, was

☐ *Hitler's famous jig which he supposedly performed before newsreel cameramen to celebrate the surrender of France was faked during processing by a Canadian film technician.*

CHAPTER IV

VERBS AND VERBAL PHRASES

	UNIT 1 VERBS
is	*The riding academy is down the street.* The verb in this sentence is _____.
drove	☐ The predicate of every sentence contains at least one verb, a word that expresses either action or state of being. *John drove.* The predicate of this sentence is the verb _____, a word that expresses action.
ran *felt*	☐ A verb can also express state of being. *He felt good after he ran.* This sentence contains two verbs. One of them, _____, expresses action; the other, _____, expresses state of being.

□   *Tom is here.*

The verb in this sentence is *is*. The eight forms of the verb *be* (*am, are, is, was, were, be, being, been*) do not express an action but rather the _____
state of being
_____ of the subject.

□ To review, then, a verb is any word that expresses
action   predicate
_____ or state of being. The _____
of every sentence contains at least one verb.

□   *He worked late.*
     He was tired.

The verbs in these sentences are *worked* and *was*. The
worked
verb _____ expresses action; the verb
was
_____ expresses state of being.

□ We can always identify verbs because only verbs have a form to indicate past time. *Went* is such a form of *go*;
drive
drove is such a form of _____.

□ The form of the verb *drink* which indicates past time is
drank
_____.

□   *bring   ask   newspaper*
     however   within   give

By asking which of the words in this list have a form to
bring   ask
indicate past time, we can see that only some of them
give
can be verbs. Identify which ones they are.

□   *John usually sleeps well, but he becomes restless if there is*
     noise in the house.

Identify the verbs in this sentence. Remember that verbs
sleeps   becomes
are those words which are used to express action or state
is
of being and which have a form to indicate past time.

Identify the verbs in the following sentences.

leave

☐ *We leave tomorrow.*

delivers

☐ *The postman delivers our mail by truck.*

is

☐ *He is here now.*

runs   circles
contains

☐ *The belt runs through this loop here and circles the section of the motor which contains the carburetor.*

UNIT 2   CONSISTENCY OF TENSE

Replace any incorrect words in the following sentences.

comes
~~came~~
kills
~~killed~~

After Beowulf slays the monster Grendel, he believes that the countryside is safe. However, on the night following, Grendel's mother came to the warriors' hall seeking revenge and killed one of Hrothgar's great chieftains.

☐ Verbs have two basic forms to indicate time, or tense: the present tense and the past tense. *Discover* is a verb in the present tense; *discovered* is a verb in the _____.

past tense

☐ Problems in tense arise if we ignore the logical relationship between two or more verbs in a sentence.

He leaves the paper when he goes to work.

Since the two actions expressed are connected in the present time, both the verb *leaves* of the main clause and the verb _____ of the subordinate clause are in the _____ tense.

goes
present

☐   *He left the paper when he [go] to work.*

Since the verb *left* is now in the _____ tense, we must complete the sentence with the form of the bracketed verb in the same tense, _____.

past

went

69

□   *He left the paper when he went to work.*

is

Went, the past tense of the verb in the subordinate clause, (is, is not) logical because the two actions are connected in a past time.

□ Replace the incorrect verb in this sentence with its correct form.

ran

~~runs~~

When I asked him to stop, he runs away.

□ If we choose the present tense in telling a story or discussing ideas, we should use the present tense consistently in a sentence or a sequence of related sentences.

*Othello's extreme jealousy leads him to kill Desdemona.
His realization of Iago's trickery came too late.*

comes

Since *leads* is in the present tense, consistency requires that we change *came* to its present-tense form, _____.

□   *The writer lists a number of grave dangers in growing inflation.
His article, however, contained few suggestions for its remedy.*

contained   contains

To make the tense of this sentence sequence correct, we must replace the verb _____ with _____.

□ Whether we choose the present or past tense in telling a story or discussing an idea, we should be consistent. Cross out and replace the incorrect verbs in this sentence sequence.

watched

~~watches~~

decided

~~decides~~

During the talk the crowd became restless. Mr. Zimmer watches the audience uneasily and decides to end the talk immediately. His presence of mind saved the situation from becoming dangerous.

70

□ Cross out and replace the incorrect verbs in this sentence sequence.

speaks
~~spoke~~
drops
~~dropped~~

Jordan Baker, one of Fitzgerald's most memorable characters, appears at the party along with the others. Nick spoke to her, and then she dropped from his sight in the crowd of moving figures.

Choose the correct verb to complete this sentence.

rises

The father told his child that the sun always [rises, rose] in the East.

□ Usually, we express any general rule such as a law of nature or a person's normal habits with a present-tense verb.

Oil floats on water.
Oil covered the water and beaches.

first

Only the (first, second) sentence is a general rule.

□ When expressing a general rule, we are not concerned with time. Therefore, we use the present tense, no matter what the tense of related verbs in the sentence is. Complete this sentence.

boils

We knew that water [boils, boiled] at a lower temperature in the mountains.

□ Choose the correct form to complete this sentence.

is
gives

Madame Curie discovered that radium [is, was] an element that [gives, gave] off particles of energy.

□ Make sure that the following sentences do or do not deal with a general rule before completing them.

divide

The instructor explained that single-cell animals [divide, divided] to reproduce themselves.

The students watched through their microscopes while a
divided
group of tiny single-cell animals [divide, divided].

71

Complete the following sentences.

exists

☐ *The lecturer explained why he doubted that life [exists, existed] on Mars at the present time.*

goes

☐ *In a copyrighted article, Paul Dillon expresses his belief that a two-party system is not only desirable but necessary. He [goes, went] on to show how a single-party system can lead to dictatorship.*

covers

☐ *It was well known in the eighteenth century that the ocean [covers, covered] three-quarters of the earth's surface.*

UNIT 3   ACTIVE AND PASSIVE VERBS

Rewrite this sentence, changing the verb to the passive voice.

The canary was fed by William.

William fed the canary.

_____

☐ Verbs have a quality called voice. This term refers to the two forms of verbs that allow us to show whether the subject acts or receives the action.

> *I see the audience.*
> *I am seen by the audience.*

first
second

In the (first, second) sentence the subject *I* acts. In the (first, second) sentence, the subject *I* receives the action of the verb.

☐ If the subject of a sentence acts, the verb is in the active voice.

> *The winner bowled a perfect game.*

active
winner

The verb *bowled* is in the _____ voice because it expresses an action of the subject, _____.

72

□ If the subject receives the action, the verb is in the passive voice.

A perfect game was bowled by the winner.

In this sentence the subject *game* receives the action; the two-part verb *was bowled* is in the passive _____.

voice

□ We form the passive voice with the appropriate form of *be* plus an action verb.

The meeting was recently canceled.

The passive voice of the verb in this sentence is formed with *was* plus the action verb _____.

canceled

□   *The hunter was killed by a stray bullet.*
       A stray bullet killed the hunter.

The verb in the first sentence is in the _____ voice; the verb in the second is in the _____ voice.

passive
active

□ Rewrite this sentence, changing the verb to the passive voice.

The Hudsons bought a new stereo console.

_____.

A new stereo console
was bought by the
Hudsons.

□ Rewrite this sentence, changing the verb to the active voice.

An important game was won by Syracuse.

_____.

Syracuse won an
important game.

Bob was given a new assignment by Dr. Kenworth.
Dr. Kenworth gave Bob a new assignment.

The (first, second) sentence is more direct and concise because its verb is in the _____ voice.

second
active

73

□ Notice that changing an active verb to a passive verb requires a change in the subject of a sentence.

> *The carpenter added four rooms.*
> *Four rooms were added by the carpenter.*

The carpenter
Four rooms

The subject of the first sentence is _____. The subject of the second is _____.

□ In a sentence with a passive verb, the real actor is never the subject but is the object of a preposition, *by*.

> *The economic outlook was outlined by the president.*
> *The president outlined the economic outlook.*

the president
second

In both sentences the actor related to the verb *outlined* is _____ but the subject only of the (first, second).

□ Making the real actor the object of the preposition *by* instead of the subject places the actor in a secondary position grammatically. This shift may weaken the expressive power of a sentence.

> *The rich are often envied by the poor.*
> *The poor often envy the rich.*

second
active

The (first, second) sentence is more direct and concise because the verb is in the _____ voice.

□ We should be careful not to use a passive verb unless it is necessary.

> *A corsage was brought to Helen by her date.*

This sentence is obviously weak because it uses a passive verb unnecessarily. Rewrite it, changing the verb to the active voice.

date brought her
a corsage

> *Helen's* _____.

□   *A long double to deep center field was smashed by*
       Sanchez.
       Robinson fielded the ball and threw quickly to third.

Rewrite the weaker sentence of these two so that it is as direct and concise as the other.

Sanchez smashed a long double to deep center field.

_____

□ Notice that in sentences with a passive verb, we can omit the actor entirely.

   The tree was cut down by the workers.
   The tree was cut down.

Omitting the actor from the second sentence (does, does not) make it grammatically incomplete.

does not

□ Although we should avoid using the passive voice, it is useful if we do not know who or what acts because we can omit mention of the actor.

   The wheel was devised long before recorded history.
   Mexico was conquered by Cortez.

Only one of these sentences can be changed to the active voice because the actor is mentioned, the (first, second).

second

□   *Five valuable furs were stolen from the home of Helen*
       Gardiner.

If the thief is unknown, we can give this sentence a verb in the active voice only by using a vague and complicated subject such as *some person or persons.*

   Some person or persons stole five valuable furs from the
   home of Helen Gardiner.

Obviously the passive voice is better than the active voice if the real actor (is, is not) known.

is not

□ *Someone or something broke our picture window during our absence.*

Since the real actor, the person or thing that broke the window, is unknown, this sentence would be better if its verb were in the passive voice and the vague subject, *Someone or something,* were omitted.

was broken

Our picture window _____ *during our absence.*

□ *Someone must have given Bob incorrect instructions.*
Mr. Hopkins gave Bob incorrect instructions.

One of these sentences would be better with its verb in the passive voice. Rewrite it.

Bob must have been given incorrect instructions.

_____

□ The passive voice is also useful if the real actor is unimportant.

Automobiles, flash floods, a tornado, an exploding boiler, and a misplaced stepladder injured five hundred persons over the holiday weekend.

The writer's use of the active voice in this sentence obliged him to list all the possible causes of injury. If he listed them realizing they were unimportant to his story but wishing to use the active voice, he burdened his reader and himself unnecessarily. This sentence would be far more concise with the verb in the passive voice and with the real actors unexpressed.

were injured

Five hundred people _____ *over the holiday weekend.*

active
passive
passive

□ Since the _____ voice is generally more direct and concise than the _____ voice, we should not employ the _____ voice without good reason.

unimportant
will not

□ In most instances, we choose the passive voice if the real actor is unknown or _____. In these instances, the real actor (will, will not) be expressed.

76

Rewrite any sentence below which can be improved by a change in voice. Mark good sentences C.

☐ *China was once called Cathay.*

_____

C

_____

Mr. Jones mixed the
paint carefully and
applied it to the
undercoated panels.

☐ *The paint was mixed carefully by Mr. Jones and applied by him to the undercoated panels.*

_____

The Giants' two starting
tackles were injured
during yesterday's
scrimmage.

☐ *Someone or something injured the Giants' two starting tackles during yesterday's scrimmage.*

_____

_____

UNIT 4   AVOIDING SHIFTS IN VOICE

Although it was foggy, the Statue of Liberty was seen as we entered New York Harbor.

Although it was foggy,
we saw the Statue of
Liberty as we entered
New York Harbor.

Rewrite this sentence to correct the shift in voice.

_____

_____

☐ If we carelessly shift from the active to the passive voice, our sentences tend to be awkward and sometimes misleading.

A crash was heard as Roger entered the room.

This sentence has a shift in voice, leaving doubtful the question of who did the hearing. The first verb is in the

passive
active

_____ voice, and the second verb is in the

_____ voice.

77

☐   A crash was heard as Roger entered the room

heard a crash

Correct the shift in voice to make it clear that Roger did the hearing and the entering: *Roger* _____ _____ *as he entered the room.*

☐   *Smith stayed at his desk until the assignment was written.*

until he had written the assignment

Correcting the shift in voice will make it clear that Smith did the staying and the writing: *Smith stayed at his desk* _____.

☐ We should also avoid shifting voice in related sentences.

> *I have two tennis rackets, one heavier than the other.*
> *The heavy racket is used for practice games.*

second   active

To improve this sentence sequence, we should rewrite the (first, second) one, changing the verb to the _____ voice.

☐ Correct the shift illustrated in the last frame by rewriting the second sentence.

I use the heavy racket for practice games.

_____
_____

☐   *First, Mr. Miller mixed the powder with an equal part of solvent. When it had hardened slightly, a heavy coat was applied to the raw lumber.*

When it had hardened slightly, he applied a heavy coat to the raw lumber.

We can improve this sentence sequence by correcting the shift in voice. Rewrite the weak sentence.

_____
_____

REVIEW

Rewrite the following sentences when necessary to correct a shift in voice. Mark correct sentences C.

Dave fired hastily at the elk just as soon as he saw it.

☐   *Dave fired hastily at the elk just as soon as it was seen.*

_____
_____

C

☐ Government defense contracts exert an immense economic influence.

_____

_____

I found the scissors because my mother suggested that I look under my bed.

☐ *The scissors were found because my mother suggested that I look under my bed.*

_____

_____

Anne missed the plane because she overslept.

☐ *The plane was missed because Anne overslept.*

_____

_____

UNIT 5 DANGLING VERBAL PHRASES

If any of the following sentences has a dangling verbal phrase, underline the phrase. Mark good sentences C.

(a) *To complete the puzzle*

(b) C

(c) *Feeling better*

(a) *To complete the puzzle, the missing pieces are essential.*
(b) *Swimming furiously upstream, the fish finally reached the spawning ground.*
(c) *Feeling better, the prospects for the children's complete recovery were increasing.*

☐ If two sentences have the same subject, we can often combine them by using only the predicate of one as part of the other sentence.

He was rowing down the river. He hit a rock.
Rowing down the river, he hit a rock.

has

The last sentence (has, does not have) the same meaning as the first two combined.

☐ The predicate of one sentence used in another sentence is called a verbal phrase.

Running across the lawn, Jane tripped.

Running across the lawn

The verbal phrase in this sentence is _____

_____.

79

☐ To make a verbal phrase out of some predicates, we have to change the verb to the *-ing* form.

> *I felt happy. I left for the party.*

Complete this sentence:

Feeling

_____ *happy, I left for the party.*

☐ To make verbal phrases out of other predicates, we need to change the verb to its *to* form: *to have, to sleep, to go.*

> *We finished the job. We worked late.*

Combine these sentences.

finish the job,
we worked late

To _____.

☐ Combine these sentences, using a verbal phrase. Here we can use the verb just as it stands.

> *They were left in the sun. They melted.*

Left in the sun

_____, *they melted.*

☐ Remember that, to form a verbal phrase from some predicates, we may need to use the *-ing* or *to* form of the verb. Combine these sentences.

> *She found the children. She had to look outside.*

To find the children

_____, *she had to look outside.*

☐ Combine these sentences.

> *I arrived late. I apologized profusely to the host.*

Arriving late

_____, *I apologized profusely to the host.*

☐ We can combine sentences using a verbal phrase only if the subject we omit from the first is expressed in the second.

> *He ran after her. He caught her at the corner.*
> *He ran after her. Her friend stayed behind.*

first

We can combine only the (first, second) sentence group using a verbal phrase.

80

☐ If we make a verbal phrase out of a sentence that does not have the omitted subject in the sentence we join it with, the result is called a dangling verbal phrase.

Driving over the hill, the ocean came into view.

On first reading, this sentence seems to say that the

ocean

_____ was driving over the hill.

☐ Dangling verbal phrases cause trouble because they make a sentence hard to follow and sometimes unintentionally comic.

Wearing a pink dress, Harry was able to find her in the crowd.

is

Here the verbal phrase *Wearing a pink dress* (is, is not) dangling.

☐ Use verbal phrases only when the omitted subject is also expressed in the sentence to which it is joined.

I was going home early. I missed the traffic.
I was going home early. The traffic wouldn't slow me down.

Only one of these sentence groups can be combined:

I missed the traffic

Going home early, _____.

☐ *We stood by the tower. The bells seemed unusually loud.*
We stood by the tower. We found the bells unusually loud.

Only one of these sentence groups can be combined using a verbal phrase:

we found the bells
unusually loud

Standing by the tower, _____
_____.

☐ *To learn shorthand, practice is necessary.*
To learn shorthand, a student needs practice.

One of these sentences contains a dangling verbal phrase,

first

the (first, second).

81

□ *She remembered my birthday. She marked it on her calendar.*

She remembered my birthday. My mother, however, forgot it.

Only one of these sentences can be combined using a verbal phrase:

To remember my birthday, she marked it on her calendar.

_____

REVIEW

Underline the dangling verbals in the following sentences. Mark good sentences C.

C

□ *Tacking against the wind, the crew just missed the bell buoy.*

Writing carefully

□ *Writing carefully, the assignment was finished in time to hand in.*

To choose political candidates wisely

□ *To choose political candidates wisely, their voting records must be studied.*

Lying in bed

□ *Lying in bed, the idea sounded interesting.*

CHAPTER V

NOUNS

	He gave us four old chairs and a table.
chairs table	List the nouns in this sentence: _____

☐ The subject of a sentence names what the sentence is about, and the most important word in the subject is usually a name word called a noun.

The men left early.

The most important word in the subject of this sentence is the noun _____.

men

☐   *The books are for sale.*

The most important word in the subject of this sentence is the _____ *books.*

noun

83

☐ The term *noun* refers to any word that names a person (*Bob*), place (*Chicago*), object (*baseball*), quality (*beauty*), etc.

> *Ralph admires goodness.*

Ralph
goodness

The two nouns in this sentence are _____ and _____.

☐ Since it may not always be easy to distinguish nouns from other words, we should know that nouns change form in ways in which other words do not. For instance, nouns have a form ending in 's: *Bob's, Chicago's, baseball's, beauty's.* Thus we can say that *desk* (can, cannot) be used as a noun but that *among* (can, cannot).

can
cannot

☐ *brought*   *Ed*
   Denver   *with*
   to   *furniture*

Using the test described in the last frame, we know that only the following words from this group can be used as nouns:

Denver   Ed
furniture

_____

☐ *He gave us a bundle of used wood.*

bundle   wood

The nouns in this sentence are _____.

☐ *The team will play in the stadium.*

team   stadium

The nouns in this sentence are _____.

REVIEW

Identify all the nouns in the following sentences.

Helen   dance
Charlie

☐ *Helen came to the dance with Charlie.*

Wisdom   results
experience

☐ *Wisdom is one of the results of experience.*

84

puck ice goal	☐	*The puck slid along the ice toward the opposite goal.*

UNIT 2   VERB AGREEMENT WITH IRREGULAR NOUNS

	Charlie does his work. *The girls do theirs.*
singular *Charlie* plural *girls*	In the first sentence the verb *does* is the (singular, plural) form to agree with the subject _____. In the second sentence *do* is the (singular, plural) form to agree with the subject _____.
are	☐ The most important relationship in any sentence is that between the subject and the verb. This relationship requires that the verb agree with its subject. For instance, we say *I am here* but not *We am here*; the present-tense form of *be* which agrees with *we* is _____.
subject	☐ The subject, then, determines what form of the verb we use. In other words, the verb must agree with the _____.
singular plural	☐ The subject of a sentence may be either singular or plural. If it refers to a single person or thing, it is _____; if it refers to more than one person or thing, it is _____.
Newspapers more than one	☐ *Newspapers affect public opinion.* The subject of this sentence is the noun _____. We call it plural because it refers to (one, more than one) thing.
Al singular	☐ *Al arrives early tomorrow.* The subject of this sentence is the noun _____. We call it _____ because it refers to a single person.

□ A singular subject requires the singular form of a verb.

> *Water [freeze, freezes].*

singular

Since the subject of this sentence is singular, we must complete the sentence with *freezes*, the _____ form of the bracketed verb.

□ Singular verbs in the present tense end in *s* or *es*. The

contains
does

singular form of *contain* is _____; the singular form of *do* is _____.

□ Plural nouns as subjects require the plural form of the verb, the present-tense form without the *s*. The plural

go
receive

form of *goes* is _____; the plural form of *receives* is _____.

Choose the correct verb for each of the following sentences.

are
are
are

> *The data [is, are] complete.*
> *The alumni [is, are] here.*
> *The theses [is, are] ready.*

□ Unlike all other verbs, which have only two present-tense forms, *be* has three present-tense forms: *am* (used only with the subject *I*), *is*, and *are*.

> *One is gone; three are left.*

singular
plural

Is agrees with (singular, plural) subjects, *are* with (singular, plural) subjects.

□ In addition, *be* is the only verb that has singular and plural past-tense forms.

> *One was gone; three were left.*

was
were

The past-tense form of *be* which agrees with singular subjects is _____; the form that agrees with plural subjects is _____.

□ *Be* is the only verb that has a singular and a plural form

past

in the _____ tense, *was* and *were*.

86

□ We who speak English regularly do not need a list of rules for subject-verb agreement. We choose the correct form of a verb for a subject with little difficulty; for most of us the choice is automatic. Complete these sentences with either *fill* or *fills*.

fills

fill

> This machine _____ the bottles.
> These tubes _____ the machine.

□ However, we can choose the correct form of the verb only if we know whether the subject is singular or plural. We

singular

plural

know, for instance, that *machine* is _____ and that *tubes* is _____.

□ The majority of nouns in English have a plural form ending in *s* or *es*, but some do not. The plural of *car* is

cars   children

_____. But the plural of *child* is _____.

□ Most of the irregular plural forms of nouns are so familiar to us that we use them without being aware that they are irregular. We unconsciously recognize *men* as the plural of

man   woman

_____ and *women* as the plural of _____.

feet

□ We don't say *two foots* but rather *two* _____. Similarly, we don't say *two tooths* but rather *two*

teeth

_____.

□ Certain plural forms borrowed from Latin and Greek present difficulties because we use them less often. We may have to be careful in identifying *crises* as the plural of *crisis*. Another word formed identically is *analyses*, the

analysis

plural of _____.

□ A noun ending in *sis* would have an almost unpro-nounceable plural form if it were made by the addition of yet another *s* sound. Try to pronounce *thesis* with *es* added to it. It can be done; but because the sound is unpleasant and difficult to make clearly, we form the plural of nouns ending in *sis* by changing the *i* before the

theses

final *s* to *e*. Thus, the plural of *thesis* is _____.

□ *Hypothesis* and *basis* are two other nouns of this kind. Complete the plural formations of the incomplete words in these sentences.

hypotheses
bases

The hypothes[is, es] are given.
The bas[is, es] are clearly presented.

□ The Latin and Greek plural forms of certain nouns borrowed from these languages remain a part of English. For instance, we find *foci*, the Latin plural form of *focus*, used by a few writers. We also find *alumni*, a word similarly

alumnus

formed, used regularly as the plural of _____.

□ Also popular is the plural form *phenomena* for the noun *phenomenon*. The noun *criterion* has a similarly formed plural.

criteria

These three criteri[a, ons] are valuable aids.

□ In Latin, nouns ending in *um* have a plural formed by exchanging that ending for *a*. Consequently, we often find *curricula* as the plural form of *curriculum* and *memo-*

memorandum

randa as the plural form of _____.

□ Many of these irregular forms are now passing from the language. For instance, we often find the forms *curriculums* and *memorandums* in use. We must be aware, however, that these nouns have two plural forms in common use. *Medium* is another noun which follows this pattern.

Two influential _____ *are radio and television.*

A sentence such as this may be completed with one of

media
mediums

two plural forms of the noun *medium*: _____ or _____.

88

□ The noun *data* is the plural of the less familiar singular noun *datum*. Until recently *data* served as both a singular and plural noun, but the use of *datum* by scientists to refer to a single fact has brought the singular form into general use. Now *datum* refers to a single fact, *data* to a number of related facts. Complete these sentences.

was
were

> *That datum [was, were] important.*
> *Those data [was, were] important.*

□ Our use of the relatively few nouns with irregular forms should follow current practice. If in doubt about the form of a noun, we should consult the dictionary.

(No response
required.)

□ Complete this frame only if you have a dictionary ready at hand. Look up each word.

indexes   indices
species (identical to
the singular form)

> The noun *index* has two plural forms in general use,
> _____ and _____. The noun *species* has only one plural form, _____.

REVIEW

Complete the following sentences.

were

□ *He discovered that his major hypotheses [was, were] not supported by other findings.*

return

□ *The alumni [returns, return] every year during Homecoming Week.*

are

□ *The South American political crises [is, are] the concern of North Americans.*

was

□ *The datum [was, were] crucial.*

were

□ *His criteria [was, were] carefully stated.*

UNIT 3 VERB AGREEMENT WITH SINGULAR NOUNS HAVING PLURAL FORMS

Complete these sentences.

is

> *Mumps [is, are] among a number of mild contagious diseases.*

are

> *Statistics [is, are] sometimes misleading.*

□ Some nouns ending in *s* or *es* are plural in form but singular in meaning. If a plural form refers to a number of things considered as a unit, it requires a singular verb.

> *A thousand dollars is too much to pay.*

singular

Although plural in form, *dollars* takes the (singular, plural) verb *is* because the amount of dollars is considered a single unit.

□ Some nouns referring to numbers of things are singular or plural depending on their meaning.

> *Over three thousand orders have been mailed.*
> *Over three thousand dollars has been stolen.*

plural

In the first sentence here, *orders* is (singular, plural) because it refers to a number of separate things. In the

singular

second sentence, *dollars* is (singular, plural) because it refers to a number of things considered as a unit.

□ Complete these sentences only after you have determined whether the subject of each has a singular or a plural meaning.

seems

> *In this heat, fifteen minutes [seem, seems] like a long time.*

have

> *During today's hot weather, fifteen persons [has, have] been hospitalized.*

90

☐ Complete these sentences.

was	*Thirty thousand dollars [was, were] set aside as a sinking fund.*
are	*Thirty thousand engineers [is, are] employed by aerospace firms.*

☐ Nouns ending in *s* or *es* may be either singular or plural, depending on meaning. *News,* for instance, is a descendant of a plural word meaning novelties, but it is now considered singular.

was   *The news [was, were] frightening.*

☐ *The United States* is also normally singular.

suffers   *Like other nations, the United States [suffer, suffers] from technological unemployment.*

☐ English has several singular nouns ending in *ics—physics, mathematics,* and *economics,* for example. Normally, nouns ending in *ics* require a singular verb:

is   *Civics [is, are] the study of political responsibility.*

☐ *Civics, physics,* and similar words always refer to a subject of study, a single thing, and are therefore (singular, plural).

singular

☐ Certain commonly used nouns ending in *ics,* such as *athletics, statistics,* and *politics,* may have a singular or a plural meaning, depending on their use in a sentence.

Athletics was the subject of the debate.
Athletics are pursued with zeal in many great universities.

In the first sentence, *Athletics* refers to sports considered as a whole and requires a (singular, plural) verb. In the second sentence, *Athletics* refers to a number of sports and requires a (singular, plural) verb.

singular

plural

☐ Complete these sentences only after determining whether *Statistics* refers to a single thing or to more than one thing.

is

were

> *Statistics [is, are] taught during the fall semester.*
> *Statistics [was, were] gathered carefully.*

☐ Complete these sentences.

are

is

> *His politics [is, are] a product of careful study.*
> *Politics [is, are] seldom considered an ennobling profession.*

☐ Several singular nouns with plural forms cause difficulty because they are often given plural verbs even though they refer to only one thing. For instance, since we say *Smallpox is contagious*, we should also say *Measles*

is

> _____ *contagious.*

one

singular

☐ Although they end in *s*, *measles* and *mumps* refer to (one, more than one) thing and are, therefore, (singular, plural).

☐ Unlike *measles* and *mumps*, nouns like *scissors, pants, trousers,* and *tweezers* refer to two-part objects and normally take plural verbs.

are

are

> *The pants [is, are] mine.*
> *The scissors [is, are] dull.*

☐ Complete these sentences.

has

have

> *Mumps [has, have] broken out among the schoolchildren.*
> *The tweezers [has, have] rusted.*

REVIEW

Complete the following sentences.

need

☐ *These pinking shears [needs, need] sharpening.*

is

☐ *"Capitol Reports" [is, are] a summary of political events in Washington.*

was	☐ *Basic economics [was, were] the subject of Professor Williams' talk.*
is	☐ *Three dollars [is, are] too much to pay for that.*
were	☐ *The statistics [was, were] provided by over seventy field-workers.*

UNIT 4   VERB AGREEMENT WITH STRUCTURALLY COMPLEX SUBJECTS

	Complete these sentences.
are	*The golf clubs on the shelf in the front closet [is, are] mine.*
was	*A collection consisting of four paintings by Klee and two by Cézanne [was, were] donated to the museum.*

☐ A noun may be separated from its related verb by a number of words.

The treasurer graduates today.
The treasurer of several campus organizations graduates today.

In both these sentences, the subject is the noun

treasurer	_____.

☐ *The man who bought the tickets was late for his flight.*

The singular verb *was* does not agree with the plural noun *tickets* but with the singular noun of the subject,

man	_____.

☐ If one or more plural nouns appear between a singular subject and its verb, we might choose erroneously the plural form of the verb. We can avoid error by identifying the subject before choosing the verb.

> One of the ten switches on the four panels [turns, turn] on a separate light.

One
turns

The subject of this sentence is _____. The correct form of the verb is _____.

☐ Another common mistake is to choose the singular form of a verb when one or more singular nouns separate it from a plural subject.

> The members of the group within the club [expect, expects] to form a committee.

expect
members

The correct form of the verb is _____ because it must agree with the subject _____.

☐ The best way to assure that the verb agrees with its subject is to tie them together mentally, ignoring all intervening words.

> Almost every member of the audience standing in the aisles remains until the performance is over.

member   remains

The subject and verb of this sentence are _____ and _____.

☐

> The team of research engineers and physicists assigned to the studies [report, reports] today.

Join the subject of this sentence mentally with each of the verb forms. The form that agrees with the subject, the

team   reports

noun _____, is _____.

<table>
<tr><td></td><td>☐ Remember also that the subject might not be the first element in a sentence.</td></tr>
<tr><td></td><td>*Of their five children only one of the older girls [is, are] courteous.*</td></tr>
<tr><td>*is*
one</td><td>The correct form of the verb is _____ because it agrees with the subject _____.</td></tr>
<tr><td></td><td>☐ Complete these sentences.</td></tr>
<tr><td>*has*</td><td>*In all these years just one of our fraternity members [has, have] played varsity football.*</td></tr>
<tr><td>*are*</td><td>*Before the flight the test engineers in charge of research and development [is, are] responsible for the fueling operation.*</td></tr>
<tr><td></td><td>Complete these sentences.</td></tr>
<tr><td>*is*</td><td>*There [is, are] only one of several solutions given in the book.*</td></tr>
<tr><td>*are*</td><td>*Here [is, are] the only three tickets I could get.*</td></tr>
<tr><td></td><td>☐ We often introduce a form of *be* with *there*. When identifying the subject of sentences having this pattern, remember that *there* is never the subject.</td></tr>
<tr><td></td><td>*There are three lamps in the room.*
Three lamps are in the room.</td></tr>
<tr><td>*lamps*</td><td>The pattern of these sentences is different, but both have the same subject, the plural noun _____.</td></tr>
<tr><td></td><td>☐   *There are three lamps in the room.*</td></tr>
<tr><td>*after*</td><td>When *there* introduces a form of *be,* the subject of the sentence comes (before, after) the verb.</td></tr>
<tr><td></td><td>☐   *There was one problem remaining to be solved.*</td></tr>
<tr><td>*was*
problem</td><td>The singular verb _____ introduced by *There* agrees with the singular subject _____.</td></tr>
</table>

	☐ *There [has, have] been in all only one satisfying method.*
method *has*	Since the subject of this sentence is _____, a singular noun, the correct form of the verb is _____.
	☐ Similarly, we sometimes introduce a form of *be* with the adverb *here*. Like *there*, *here* cannot be the subject of a sentence.
	Here are the tickets.
tickets	The subject of this sentence is not *Here* but the plural noun _____.
	☐ *Here [is, are] the men who will move the piano.*
men *are*	Since the verb must agree with the subject _____, the correct form is _____.
	☐ Complete these sentences.
is *were*	*There [is, are] the first tennis racquet I ever owned.* *Here [was, were] the two people he admired the most.*
	Complete these sentences.
arrive *is*	*Mr. Wilson and his son [arrives, arrive] tomorrow.* *Either the committee members or the mayor [is, are] responsible.*
	☐ Some subjects are compound; that is, they have two or more parts joined by a conjunction such as *and* or *or*.
	Salt and pepper are the most common seasonings.
Salt *pepper*	The compound subject of this sentence consists of two singular nouns, _____ and _____.

□ Even though each element joined by *and* in a compound subject is singular, the whole subject is plural because it refers to more than one thing.

> *Hiking and swimming [is, are] favorite pastimes.*

and

are

Since the parts of the compound subject in this sentence are joined by _____, the correct form of the verb is _____.

□ A compound subject joined by *and* may, of course, have more than two singular elements.

> *Baseball, basketball, and football [is, are] popular spectator sports.*

are

Even though each of the three nouns of the compound subject in the sentence is singular, the correct form of the verb is _____.

□ Like *and, or* may join more than two elements in a compound subject. However, if the elements are singular, the verb must be singular, no matter how many elements the subject contains.

fits

> *A table, a chair, or a bookcase [fits, fit] into this space.*

□ If all the elements joined by *or* in a compound subject are plural, the verb must, of course, be plural.

> *Days, weeks, or even months [passes, pass] as rapidly as a minute.*

plural   pass

Since all the elements of this compound sentence are (singular, plural), the correct form of the verb is _____.

□ Complete these sentences.

are

> *Plastic bottles, cups, or glasses [is, are] included in the basket.*

is

> *An icepick, a knife, or a nail [is, are] useful in marking leather.*

☐ A compound subject may have both a singular and a plural element joined by *or*. In such cases the verb should agree with the element nearer it.

> Five small roses or a single gardenia *[makes, make]* an attractive corsage.

makes

Since the singular noun *gardenia* is nearer the verb, the correct form is _____.

☐ A single gardenia or five small roses *[makes, make]* an attractive corsage.

roses
make

Since the plural noun _____ is nearer the verb, the correct form is _____.

☐ We often use the conjunction *or* in the correlative form *either . . . or*. The addition of *either* to *or* in a compound subject does not change the principles of agreement.

> Either he or she *[was, were]* there all day.
> He or she *[was, were]* there all day.

was

The correct verb for both sentences is _____.

☐ Complete this sentence.

> Either apples or pears *[is, are]* served for dessert.

are

☐ Another correlative form used in compound subjects is *neither . . . nor*. When choosing a verb to agree with a compound subject having this correlative, follow the same principles that apply to subjects having *or* or *either . . . or*.

> Neither Mr. Blake nor Mr. Shaw *[was, were]* here.
> Either Mr. Blake or Mr. Shaw *[was, were]* here.

was   singular

Since the separate elements of both subjects of these sentences are singular, the correct form of the verb for both is _____, the (singular, plural) form.

98

☐ These principles of subject-verb agreement apply to compound subjects whose elements are joined by *or, either . . . or,* and *neither . . . nor*: if the separate elements of the compound subject are singular, the verb must be (singular, plural); if the separate elements are plural, the verb must be (singular, plural).

singular
plural

☐ *In the beginning of the play neither characters nor incidents [is, are] convincing.*

Because the separate elements of this compound subject are (singular, plural) the correct verb is _____.

plural   *are*

☐ *Neither the trees nor the solitary cloud [seems, seem] real.*

The compound subject in this sentence is composed of a singular and a plural noun. Since the noun closer to the verb is (singular, plural), the correct verb is _____.

singular   *seems*

☐ Complete this sentence.

Neither the foreman nor the other jury members [was, were] ready to reach a decision.

were

☐ Complete these sentences.

Either the owner or his two assistants [has, have] been here.

have

Either the apples or the watermelon [is, are] enough for the picnic lunch.

is

REVIEW

Complete the following sentences.

has

☐ *One of the twenty boats in the offshore fishing fleets [has, have] a radar-equipped bridge.*

are

☐ *Here [is, are] the four team members.*

were

☐ *Neither the cheese dip nor the crackers [was, were] fresh.*

is

☐ *There [is, are] a large number of empty seats in the front of the auditorium.*

CHAPTER VI

PRONOUNS

UNIT 1   PRONOUNS: PERSON

(a) second	(e) third
(b) third	(f) first
(c) first	(g) third
(d) third	(h) third

Identify the following words according to person.

(a) you _____   (e) boat _____

(b) she _____   (f) I _____

(c) we _____   (g) it _____

(d) each _____   (h) he _____

☐ Pronouns are name words like nouns; but unlike nouns, pronouns refer to someone or something that they do not specifically name.

I dislike liver.

Instead of using his own name, the speaker refers to himself with the pronoun _____.

I

you
he

□   *Do you know whether he likes liver?*

This sentence contains two pronouns; the pronoun referring to the person spoken to is _____; the
pronoun referring to the person spoken about is _____.

□ One way we identify pronouns is by person. Those that
refer to (or include) the person speaking are of the first
person.

I told him we will be there.

The two first-person pronouns in this sentence are

I   we
_____ and _____.

□ Pronouns of the second person refer to those who are
second
spoken to. *You* is a pronoun of the _____
person.

□ The third person includes all pronouns that refer to
someone or something spoken about.

He told me it was ready.

The two pronouns of the third person in this sentence are

He   it
_____ and _____.

□ First-person pronouns refer to (or include) the person
speaking
_____. Second-person pronouns refer to the
to
person spoken _____. Third-person pronouns
about
refer to the person or thing spoken _____.

□   *Someone gave us the book you forgot.*

Identify the three pronouns in this sentence according to
person.

us
      first person: _____
you
      second person: _____
Someone
      third person: _____

101

third about	☐ The third person includes most of the pronouns in our language. *He, she, it, they, some, all, none,* and *everything* are among the many pronouns of the _____ person; all of them refer to persons and things spoken _____.
third	☐ It is not meaningful to identify nouns according to person because we use pronouns instead of nouns in referring to ourselves speaking or to the person we are speaking to. However, since nouns refer to persons or things spoken about, we can consider them as being of the _____ person.
I you *book*	☐ All nouns and pronouns, then, are identifiable according to person. *You say that I borrowed the book?* This sentence contains one noun and two pronouns: _____ is of the first person, _____ is of the second person, and _____ is of the third person.

UNIT 2   AGREEMENT IN PERSON

me ~~*you*~~	Cross out and replace any incorrect word in this sentence. *I really enjoy swimming because it makes you feel invigorated.*
I second	☐ Identifying pronouns according to person helps us to avoid illogical shifts in our writing. *I prefer movies that make you laugh.* The writer of this sentence shifted illogically from the first-person pronoun _____ to the _____-person pronoun *you*.
first	☐ *I prefer movies that make me laugh.* This sentence is logical because both the pronouns *I* and *me* are of the (first, second) person.

102

first we second you	☐ *From where we stood you could see Mt. Shasta.* This writer begins his sentence with the _____-person pronoun _____. He then shifts illogically to the _____-person pronoun _____.
you we	☐ *From where we stood you could see Mt. Shasta.* To improve this sentence, we would replace the pronoun _____ with the pronoun _____.
you I	☐ *I should buy a map because you could get lost without one.* We can improve this sentence by replacing the pronoun _____ with the pronoun _____.
us ~~you~~	☐ Correct the error in this sentence. *We liked the extended tour because the guides let you take several side trips.*
antecedent he	*The chemist worked late in the laboratory; he did not return home until after eleven o'clock.* *Chemist* is the _____ of the pronoun _____.
Carl	☐ A pronoun of the third person usually refers to a word which precedes it. *Carl came late, but he left early.* The pronoun *he* in this sentence refers to the noun _____.
antecedent	☐ The word to which a pronoun refers is its antecedent. *Carl came late, but he left early.* In this sentence *Carl* is the _____ of *he*.

☐   *A boy can complete the test if he tries.*

In this sentence *boy* is the _____ of the pronoun _____.

antecedent
he

☐   *Peter can come provided he warns the office in advance.*

In this sentence _____ is the antecedent of the
pronoun _____.

Peter
he

---

he or she
~~*they*~~

Correct this sentence.

> *If anyone wishes a copy, they can have one.*

☐ A pronoun must agree with its antecedent in person.

> *If anyone goes out in this weather, you should wear a
> hat.*

The pronoun *you* does not agree with its antecedent
anyone because *you* is of the _____ person and
anyone is of the _____ person.

second
third

☐ Normally we use the third-person pronouns *he (him)* and
she (her) to agree with *one, anyone, anybody,* or *person*
because these are also of the third person.

> *If anyone goes out in this weather, you should wear a
> hat.*

he or she
~~*you*~~

Correct this sentence by crossing out the incorrect pronoun and replacing it with the correct one.

☐ Correct the error in this sentence.

> *When a person is applying for a job, you should be well
> dressed.*

he or she
~~*you*~~

☐ Using *he or she* in such situations, however, is cumber-
some. A better way is to choose a plural noun so that
they (them) can agree with it. Complete this sentence.

> *When persons are applying for a job, _____
> should be well dressed.*

they

104

□ Any antecedent whose elements are joined by *and* is plural and requires a plural pronoun or possessive. Complete this sentence.

> *Mrs. Smith told Bob and Pete to take the rattlesnake along with [him, them] when [he, they] left.*

them   they

□ A compound antecedent joined by *or, either . . . or,* or *neither . . . nor* is singular if its elements are singular. Complete this sentence.

> *Neither the spaniel nor the pointer could be judged until [it, they] demonstrated [its, their] abilities in the hunting events.*

it   its

□ If both elements of a compound antecedent joined by *or, either . . . or, neither . . . nor* are plural, the pronoun or possessive must be plural to agree with it.

> *Neither the owners nor the team members were pleased with [his or her, their] club's performance in the series.*

their

□ Complete these sentences.

> *Mr. Elliott and John remembered to bring [his, their] own money. However, neither Mr. Elliott nor John wanted to spend all [his, their] savings on the trip.*

their

his

□ Complete these sentences.

> *You can expect the detergent or the solvent to do [its, their] work rapidly.*
> *You can expect the detergent and the solvent to do [its, their] work rapidly.*

its

their

Mrs. Roberts handed her coat to Helen.
or
Mrs. Roberts handed Helen's coat to her.

Mrs. Roberts handed Helen her coat.

Rewrite this sentence to clarify the ambiguous reference.

_____

_____

□ Our use of a pronoun or possessive will be ambiguous unless it refers clearly to its antecedent.

Mr. Tichenor gave Jim his pencil.

We cannot tell whose pencil Mr. Tichenor gave Jim because *his* can refer either to _____ or to _____.

Mr. Tichenor
Jim

□ Sentences which have two or more possible antecedents preceding a pronoun or possessive are confusing. It is best to rewrite such sentences so that the pronoun or possessive has only one possible antecedent preceding it. Complete the revision below.

Mr. Tichenor gave Jim his pencil.
Mr. Tichenor _____ *to Jim.*

gave his pencil

□   *Mr. Tichenor gave his pencil to Jim.*

It is clear now that the pencil belongs to _____.

Mr. Tichenor

□   *The committee members submitted questions to the congressmen about their voting duties.*

This sentence is ambiguous. Because *their* can refer either to the _____ or to the _____, we cannot tell whose voting duties the questions are about.

committee members
congressmen

□   *The committee members submitted questions to the congressmen about their voting duties.*

If the voting duties are the committee members', the sentence will be clear if *their* has only the one antecedent preceding it:

The committee members submitted questions _____ _____.

about their voting duties
to the congressmen

□   *The oil will not lubricate the engine if its temperature is too high.*

This sentence is not clear because *its* has two possible antecedents, _____ and _____.

oil   engine

110

□   *The oil will not lubricate the engine if its temperature is too high.*

If *its* in this sentence refers to oil, we can rewrite the sentence this way:

the oil

the engine

    If the temperature of _____ is too high, it will not lubricate _____ .

□   *The oil will not lubricate the engine if its temperature is too high.*

If *its* refers to *engine*, we can rewrite the sentence this way:

the engine

the oil

    If the temperature of _____ is too high, _____ will not lubricate it.

    Although the car's windshield was cracked, it was safe to drive.

Rewrite this sentence correctly.

its windshield was

cracked, the car

    Although _____ was safe to drive.

□ Pronouns and possessives refer to nouns or pronouns, not modifiers or possessive forms of nouns.

    Randy tried to hold the bull's tail, but it kicked him anyway.

Since we expect *it* to refer to the noun *tail* rather than the possessive form *bull's* which modifies *tail*, this sentence

tail

seems to mean that the bull's _____ rather than the bull kicked Randy.

□   *Randy tried to hold the bull's tail, but it kicked him anyway.*

Since the antecedent cannot be the possessive form of the noun, we can correct the reference problem in this sentence by changing *bull's* to *bull* and *it* to *its*:

the bull

    Randy tried to hold its tail, but _____ kicked him anyway.

□   *In Kerr's article "The Multiversity," he discusses the crisis facing American universities.*

Since *he* cannot refer to *Kerr's*, we should substitute *his* for *he* and *Kerr* for *Kerr's*, changing their positions in the sentence:

his   *Kerr*

     In _____ article "The Multiversity," _____ discusses the crisis facing American universities.

□   *Jim recharged the car's battery even though it had four flat tires.*

Rewrite this sentence to clarify the reference of *it*. Follow the pattern used in the last three frames.

its battery even though the car

     Jim recharged _____ _____ had four flat tires.

□   *Who, whose, whom, which,* and *that* introducing relative clauses have antecedents.

     This is the car that I bought.

car

That introducing the relative clause *that I bought* has a noun for its antecedent, _____.

□   *Who, whose, whom, which,* or *that* should have a noun antecedent, never a possessive form of a noun used to identify another noun.

     Joe's wife, whom I played football with in college, is quite attractive.

Joe's wife

Joe

Since we expect *whom* to have a noun as its antecedent, this sentence seems to suggest that _____ rather than _____ played football in college.

□   *Joe's wife, whom I played football with in college, is quite attractive.*

To correct the ambiguity in this sentence, we must rearrange its parts so that *whom* has *Joe* rather than *Joe's* for its antecedent.

     Joe, whom I played football with in college, has _____ _____.

an attractive wife

	☐ *We met the senator's children, who spoke so ably before the congressional committee yesterday.*
	Rewrite this sentence to clarify the reference of *who*.
of the senator who	*We met the children* _____ *spoke so ably before the congressional committee yesterday.*
	☐ *The truck's headlights which had been driven into the field lighted up the roadway.*
	Clarify the reference of *which*.
headlights of the truck	*The* _____ *which had been driven into the field lighted up the roadway.*
	Actors have to work hard because it is a demanding profession.
	Rewrite this sentence correctly.
because acting is a demanding profession	*Actors have to work hard* _____.
	☐ Pronouns must have logical antecedents.
	Because my father is an engineer, I decided to study it.
	The antecedent of *it* in this sentence can be only *engineer*. However, a person does not study "engineer" but rather
engineering	_____.
	☐ *Because my father is an engineer, I decided to study it.*
	A pronoun lacking a logical antecedent must be replaced with the appropriate noun.
	Because my father is an engineer, I decided to study
engineering	_____.
	☐ *The Mexicans are happy even though it has a low average national income.*
	Clarifying this sentence requires this substitution:
Mexico	*The Mexicans are happy even though* _____ _____ *has a low average national income.*

□   *Although doctors are often overworked, it is a rewarding profession.*

Correct the pronoun error in this sentence.

medicine is

Although doctors are often overworked, _____ a rewarding profession.

Bob will ask the managers to support his plan, which I think is foolish.

two

The problem with this sentence is that *which* has (no, two) antecedent(s).

□ We sometimes use the pronouns *which* and *this* to refer to a whole idea rather than to a word.

   Sheila gave her month's allowance to charity, which I think was courageous.

Sheila gave her month's allowance to charity

In this sentence *which* refers to the fact that _____ _____.

□ Using *which* or *this* to refer to a whole idea may cause confusion.

   The group argued for the conservative policy; this is unrealistic.

A person reading this sentence may well ask what is unrealistic—the group's arguing or the _____.

conservative policy

□   *The group argued for the conservative policy; this is unrealistic.*

If the writer considers the arguing unrealistic, he or she should have written the sentence this way:

to argue for the conservative policy

   It was unrealistic of the group _____ _____.

☐ *The group argued for the conservative policy; this is unrealistic.*

If the writer considers the conservative policy unrealistic, he or she should have written the sentence this way:

The group argued for the _____

_____ .

unrealistic conservative policy

☐ *He announced the committee's decision publicly, which the members think was unjust.*

If the members consider the public announcement rather than the decision unjust, this sentence should be phrased this way:

The members think that it was _____

_____ .

unjust for him to announce the committee's decision publicly

REVIEW

Complete the following frames.

☐ Correct this sentence.

French
~~*it*~~

Since Lydia wished to converse while she was in France, she decided to study it.

☐ Correct this sentence.

its
~~*the radio's*~~
the radio
~~*it*~~

Although the radio's battery is weak, it still plays.

☐ *I told Bob that I had not placed his name on the roster; this was my mistake.*

If the mistake was the telling, this sentence can be clarified by rewriting it this way:

My mistake _____

_____ .

was telling [to tell] Bob that I had not placed his name on the roster

☐ Rewrite this sentence to show clearly that it is her own coat that Marianne is giving.

Marianne gave her coat to Barbara.

> *Marianne gave Barbara her coat.*
> _____

☐ Correct this sentence.

its
~~their~~

> *Neither the cola nor the root beer has saccharin in their formula.*

UNIT 5   CASE

Identify the following pronouns according to case.

(a) subjective

(b) objective

(c) subjective or
  objective

(d) subjective or
  objective

(e) objective

(f) subjective

(a) *I* _____

(b) *us* _____

(c) *you* _____

(d) *it* _____

(e) *him* _____

(f) *they* _____

☐ Personal pronouns—those referring to persons—have different forms to refer to the same person.

> *I hit the ball.*
> *The ball hit me.*

me

The pronoun *I*, the subject of the first sentence, refers to the same person as the pronoun _____, the direct object of the second sentence.

☐ The form of the pronoun depends on its function.

> *I hit the ball.*
> *The ball hit me.*

subject
object

The form *I* is used as the _____ of the first sentence. The form *me* is used as the direct _____ of the second sentence.

116

□ We distinguish the forms of personal pronouns by case. The form of the pronoun used as the subject of a sentence is said to be in the subjective case.

> *I hit the ball.*

subjective   *I* is a pronoun in the _____ case.

□ The form of the pronoun used as an object is said to be in the objective case.

> *The ball hit me.*

case   *Me* is a pronoun in the objective _____.

subjective   □ A pronoun used as a subject is in the _____ case.

objective   □ A pronoun used as an object is in the _____ case.

□
> *We thanked Sue.*
> *Sue thanked us.*

subjective
objective   *We* is in the _____ case. *Us* is in the _____ case.

subjective
objective   □ We can easily identify a pronoun according to its case by trying it as the subject or object of a verb such as *thanked*. Thus *he, she,* and *they* are in the _____ case; *him, her,* and *them* are in the _____ case.

□ The personal pronoun *you* has the same form for both the subjective and objective cases.

> *Bob thanked you.*
> *You thanked Bob.*

objective
subjective   We know from its position rather than its form that *you* in the first sentence is in the _____ case, while in the second sentence it is in the _____ case.

□ The pronoun *it*, like *you*, lacks a distinctive form for the subjective and objective cases.

> *You hit it.*
> *It hit you.*

These sentences show that both the pronoun _____ and the pronoun _____ lack distinctive subjective and objective forms.

you   it

□ Like *you* and *it*, all nouns and pronouns except the personal pronouns lack a distinctive subjective and objective form. When we speak of the subjective and objective cases, we are concerned only with the _____ pronouns—excluding *you* and *it*.

personal

REVIEW

In the following sentences identify the personal pronouns according to case.

I is subjective
him is objective

□ *I found him sleeping.*

she is subjective

□ *On the whole, she was quite uneasy.*

They is subjective
you is objective

□ *They gave you a book.*

UNIT 6   CHOOSING PRONOUN FORMS

Complete these sentences.

me

> *Just between you and [I, me], his case is hopeless.*

we

> *Neither the Carsons nor [we, us], unless there is a change in plans, can come.*

118

☐ Ordinarily we do not have to think about the case of personal pronouns in order to choose the correct form. Complete this sentence.

I   her   she
me

> *[I, me] gave [she, her] one of the books, and [she, her] returned it to [I, me] today.*

☐ One of the few difficulties we may have is in choosing the correct case of a pronoun which is part of a compound sentence element.

> *He and I came.*

He
I

Both the pronouns in this sentence, _____ and _____, are part of a compound sentence element joined by *and*.

☐ Choosing pronouns for compound elements often is troublesome because sentences containing them seem more complicated than they really are. Although we never hear *Him came* or *Me came,* we sometimes hear *Him and me came.* The correct pronouns for this sentence are these:

He   I

> _____ and _____ came.

☐   *He and I came.*

The subjective pronouns *He* and *I* are correct because both are (subjects, objects) of the verb *came.*

subjects

☐ We may also hear sentences such as this one:

> *Frank told he and I the story.*

We know that the pronouns in this sentence are incorrect because we would say neither *Frank told he the story* nor *Frank told I the story.* The correct pronouns are these:

> *Frank told _____ and _____ the story.*

him   me

☐   *Frank told him and me the story.*

Because *him and me* is an indirect object in this sentence, the (subjective, objective) pronouns *him* and *me* are correct.

objective

119

☐ *Between you and I, the party was a waste of time.*

The two pronouns in this sentence are the objects of the preposition *Between.* We would correct this sentence by substituting the pronoun _____ for the incorrect pronoun _____ .

me

I

☐ If in doubt about which form of a pronoun to use in a compound sentence part, try each form by itself.

> *In his talk today the President spoke about you and [I, me].*

Since we would not say *The President spoke about I,* we should complete this sentence with the objective pronoun

me

_____ .

☐ *[We, Us] and the Snells will live here next year.*

Trying each form of the pronoun apart from its related words shows us that the correct form is _____ .

We

☐ *Mrs. Silvers won't speak to either you or [she, her].*

We should not let the correlative form *either . . . or* hide the fact that both pronouns in this sentence are objects of the preposition *to.* The correct pronoun to complete this sentence is _____ .

her

☐ Complete this sentence.

him

> *Roger will ask either Mr. James or [he, him] to accompany us.*

Complete these sentences.

me

> *Let's you and [I, me] go.*

me

> *Two of us, Hank and [I, me], will go.*

120

□ We often clarify a noun's meaning by adding other nouns or pronouns to it.

Two brothers, Marty and he, leave today with the team.

brothers

The pronoun *he*, together with the noun *Marty*, clarifies the meaning of the noun _____.

□ Any noun or pronoun joined to another to clarify it is called an appositive.

Two brothers, Marty and he, leave today with the team.

appositives

The noun *Marty* and the pronoun *he* are both _____.

□ Pronouns serving as appositives rename in order to clarify the words they follow. Thus, a pronoun appositive following the subject of a sentence is parallel to the subject and should be in the subjective case.

Two brothers, Marty and he, leave today with the team.

subjective

Since *brothers* is the subject, the appositive pronoun *he*, in the _____ case, is correct.

□ If in doubt about which case of a pronoun to use as an appositive, substitute the pronoun by itself for the noun which it clarifies.

Their parents gave the boys, Paul and [he, him], an old car to use.

him

By trying *he* and *him* as substitutes for *the boys*, we can easily determine that the correct form is _____.

□ Complete this sentence.

me

They nominated two new members, Harry and [I, me].

121

□ Occasionally we join a pronoun directly to a noun so that both have a clearer meaning.

We men are ready.

This sentence has a subject composed of the pronoun _____ and the noun _____.

We   men

□   *We men are ready.*

subjective

Since it is part of the subject, the (subjective, objective) pronoun *We* is the correct form.

□ Pronouns joined to nouns should be in the case that they would be if they stood without the noun.

The Liptons gave [we, us] fellows a lift.

Mentally omitting the noun *fellows* shows us that the correct pronoun for this sentence is _____.

us

□ Omit the noun following the pronoun to determine which form to use in completing these sentences.

us

Some of [we, us] students studied late last night.

we

Some teachers seem to feel that [we, us] students should study late every night.

REVIEW

Correct the following sentences where necessary. Mark correct sentences C.

C

□ *It should have taken both of them.*

he
~~him~~

□ *Three members, Harry, Bob, and him, were fined for skipping meetings.*

me
~~I~~

□ *Just between you and I, Rita is a bore.*

We
~~Us~~

□ *Us girls have formed a basketball team.*

122

Who *Whom*	Complete these sentences. *[Who, Whom] do you think will win?* *[Who, Whom] do you want to win the game?*

	☐ The pronouns *who* and *whom* are also personal pronouns. If used in questions, they are called interrogative pronouns.
	Who is coming?
Who	The subject of this sentence is the interrogative pronoun _____.
	☐ The interrogative pronouns have a distinguishable form for each case. *Who* is subjective; *whom* is objective.
	Who is coming?
subjective	To show that the interrogative pronoun *who* is the subject, it is in the _____ case.
	☐ The objective form *whom* is slowly disappearing from spoken English, but in the more formal kinds of written English the distinction between *who* and *whom* is still maintained by some writers and teachers.
	To [who, whom] are you speaking?
whom	In this sentence the objective pronoun _____ is the formally correct form because it is the object of the preposition *To.*
	☐ Interrogative pronouns, both subjective and objective, always come before the verb in a sentence. For this reason we may mistake an object for the subject of the sentence.
	Whom are you speaking to?
to	The pronoun *you* is the subject of this sentence. *Whom,* the interrogative pronoun, is the object of the preposition that comes at the end of the sentence, _____.

123

□ A quick way to determine whether to use *who* or *whom* is to rephrase the question as an answer, substituting *he* or *him* for the interrogative pronoun. If *he* is correct, the question requires *who*; if *him* is correct, the question requires *whom*.

> [Who, Whom] removed the battery?

We rephrase the question as an answer this way:

He
> [He, Him] removed the battery.

□   [Who, Whom] removed the battery?

Who
Since *He* is correct in this question rephrased as an answer, the correct interrogative pronoun is _____.

□ Use the device described in the last two frames to complete these sentences.

Who
Whom
> [Who, Whom] will play in his place?
> [Who, Whom] will the coach pick to play in his place?

□ In our informal conversation we may often use *who* in place of *whom* because it sounds less stilted.

> [Who, Whom] are you referring to?
> [Who, Whom] asked her to come?

second
first
In the (first, second) sentence *Who* is both formally and informally correct. In the (first, second) sentence *Who* is correct in informal conversation.

□ Complete these sentences with the form of the pronoun customary in formal writing.

Who
Whom
> [Who, Whom] helped Mrs. Green?
> [Who, Whom] did you see helping Mrs. Green?

REVIEW

Choose the formally preferred pronoun to complete the following sentences.

Whom
□ [Who, Whom] did the committee pick to act in his place?

124

Whom	☐ *[Who, Whom] should the police question in the Folger case?*
Who	☐ *[Who, Whom] do you think came early?*

UNIT 8 RELATIVES

	Complete these sentences.
who	*I'll bet I know [who, whom] the winner will be.*
who	*Harry Fish is the candidate [who, whom] we feel is the best choice.*

	☐ We use the pronouns *who* and *whom* to introduce relative clauses.
	We avoid a person who talks too much.
who talks too much	In this sentence *who* introduces the four-word relative clause _____.
	☐ *Who* and *Whom* are called relative pronouns—or just relatives—when they relate a relative clause to the main clause.
	He asked who was coming.
relative (pronoun) *who was coming*	In this sentence the _____ *who* introduces the relative clause _____.
	☐ The relatives *who* and *whom* are also subject, subjective complement, or object in the subordinate clauses they introduce.
	Peter knew who saw me.
	Peter knew whom I saw.
who	In the first sentence the relative _____ is the subject of the clause it introduces. In the second sentence
whom	the relative _____ is the direct object of the verb *saw*, even though it appears before the verb.

125

□ As is the case with interrogative pronouns, the distinction between *who* and *whom* in the relatives is maintained only in very formal writing. In such writing, *who* is the relative of the subjective case; *whom* is the relative of the objective case.

> *Peter knew who saw me.*
> *Peter knew whom I saw.*

subject

direct object

The subjective relative *who* is used in the first sentence because it is the (subject, direct object) in its clause. The objective relative *whom* is used in the second sentence because it is the (subject, direct object) of the verb *saw*.

□ Whether subject, subjective complement, or object, the relative pronoun always precedes the verb in its clause. For this reason choosing between *who* and *whom* for some sentences may be difficult.

> *Peter knew whom I saw.*

before

Normally the direct object in a sentence follows the verb. This sentence illustrates, however, that the direct object in a subordinate clause, if it is a relative, always comes (before, after) the verb.

□ In order to choose the formally correct case of a relative, it is necessary to know what function it has in its clause. Perhaps the best help is to view the clause as an independent sentence.

> *Earl writes well. He is our associate editor.*
> *Earl, who is our associate editor, writes well.*

He is

These examples show that the relative clause *who is our associate editor* can be expressed as an independent sentence, _____ *our associate editor.*

□   *Earl writes well. He is our associate editor.*
> *Earl, who is our associate editor, writes well.*

who

Changing the sentence *He is our associate editor* to a relative clause requires the substitution of the relative in the subjective case, _____, for the subjective pronoun *He*.

126

	□ *There is the girl who won the contest.*
	Changing the relative clause *who won the contest* to an independent sentence requires substituting a subjective pronoun for the subjective relative pronoun *who*:
She won	_____ the contest.
	□ *Dr. Jordan, whom I met yesterday, is the chairman of the history department.*
	Changing the subordinate clause *whom I met yesterday* to an independent sentence requires the objective pronoun:
I met him yesterday	_____.
	□ If in doubt about whether to use *who* or *whom*, test the relative clause as an independent sentence. If it requires a subjective pronoun (*he, she, they*), the relative should be *who*. If it requires an objective pronoun (*him, her, them*),
whom	the relative should be _____.
	□ *The children [who, whom] I enjoy least are playing in the flower beds.*
	Since rewriting the relative clause [*who, whom*] *I enjoy least* as an independent sentence requires the objective
them	pronoun _____, the correct relative pronoun is
whom	_____.
	□ *Mr. Hicks frowned at those [who, whom] laughed at his jokes.*
	Since rewriting the relative clause in this sentence as an independent sentence requires the (subjective, objective)
subjective	pronoun *they*, the correct relative pronoun is _____.
who	
	□ *There is the girl [who, whom] I came with.*
	Testing the relative clause as an independent sentence shows that the correct form of the relative pronoun is
whom	_____.

Correct the following sentences where necessary, using the formally preferred form of *who* or *whom*. Mark correct sentences C.

C
☐ *The people whom we remember from high school seem to have changed when we meet them later in life.*

C
☐ *This is the girl who the judges felt was the most attractive.*

whom
~~*who*~~
☐ *When he asked me who Roger was dancing with, I couldn't answer him.*

who
~~*whom*~~
☐ *You cannot always tell whom your friends are.*

CHAPTER VII

MODIFIERS

UNIT 1 ADJECTIVES

sudden ripe	*Those sudden showers drenched the ripe corn.* The adjectives in this sentence are _____ _____.
Tall	☐ Nouns and pronouns often have descriptive words related to them. *Tall peaks border the valley.* In this sentence the descriptive word _____ is related to the noun *peaks*.
adjective	☐ Descriptive words related to nouns or pronouns are called *adjectives.* *Tall peaks border the valley.* *Tall,* then, is an _____.
Dry	☐ *Dry leaves fall.* In this sentence the adjective is _____.

□ The term we use to express the relationship which an adjective has to its noun is *modify*.

> *Black cars discolor rapidly.*

In this sentence the adjective *Black* modifies the noun

cars　　　　_____.

□　　*I dislike large, noisy parties.*

large　　In this sentence the adjectives _____ and

noisy　　_____ modify the noun *parties*.

□ One important characteristic of adjectives is that they have forms to indicate more or most of the quality they express. For instance, *large* has the forms *larger* and

noisiest　　*largest. Noisy* has the forms *noisier* and _____.

□ Many adjectives indicate more with an added *er*, most with an added *est*. Thus the adjective *bright* indicates

brighter　　more of the quality by the form _____, most

brightest　　by the form _____.

□ Other adjectives indicate more or most by their use together with *more* or *most*. The adjective *beautiful*, for instance, indicates more of the quality when added to *more*: *more beautiful*. It indicates most when added to

most beautiful　　*most*: _____.

□ Adjectives, then, have two identifying characteristics. One, they modify nouns; two, they can indicate more or most of the quality they express.

> *The small child played happily.*

We know that *small* is an adjective because it modifies

child　　the noun _____ and because it has the form

smallest　　*smaller* to indicate more and the form _____ to indicate most.

	☐ *John made an accurate count.*
count	We know that *accurate* is an adjective because it r___ the noun _____ and because it can indic___
most accurate	more by the form *more accurate* and most by the for.___ _____.
restless *young* *enthusiastic*	☐ *The restless audience greeted the young speaker with* *enthusiastic cheers.*
	Underline the adjectives in this sentence.

REVIEW

	Underline the adjectives in the following sentences.
Rainy *gloomy*	☐ *Rainy days are gloomy days.*
Large *careful*	☐ *Large houseplants need careful attention when trans-* *planted.*
attractive *interesting*	☐ *She was an attractive, interesting companion.*

UNIT 2   ADVERBS

there *quickly* *then*	*The four girls left there quickly then.* The adverbs in this sentence are _____ _____.

	☐ Adjectives modify nouns. Adverbs, the other large class of modifiers, modify verbs.
	He ran rapidly.
verb	In this sentence the adverb *rapidly* modifies the _____ *ran.*

finished

□ You may have learned that adverbs modify adjectives and adverbs as well as verbs. Here, however, we are concerned only with adverbs that modify verbs.

She finished easily.

Here the adverb *easily* modifies the verb _____.

beautifully

□ Characteristically adverbs end in *ly*. We can form adverbs from many adjectives by adding this ending. For instance, the adverb form of the adjective *proper* is *properly*. The adverb form of the adjective *beautiful* is _____.

adverb

□ *True* is an adjective; *truly* is an _____.

how

□ An adverb modifies by expressing *how*, *when*, or *where*.

The stream flowed rapidly.

The adverb *rapidly* modifies the verb *flowed* because it expresses _____ the stream flowed.

where
when

□ However, not all adverbs end in *ly*.

We arrived there late.

In this sentence the adverbs *there* and *late* modify the verb *arrived*. *There* expresses _____, and *late* expresses _____.

how   when
where

□ Even if it does not end in *ly*, any modifier that expresses _____, _____, or _____ is an adverb.

there

□ Since adverbs express *how*, *when*, or *where*, we have a simple substitution test to determine which words in a sentence function as adverbs. If we can replace a word with *thus*, *then*, or *there*, we know it is an adverb. For instance, in the sentence *He went outside*, we can replace the adverb *outside* with the word _____.

	☐ *He plays happily outside sometimes.*
happily [thus] *outside* [there] *sometimes* [then]	Using the substitution test described in the last frame, we can determine that the adverbs in this sentence, all modifying the verb *play*, are _____, _____, and _____.
	☐ Unlike adjectives, adverbs can often move about in a sentence.
	Rarely he / gives a party /.
can	The adverb *Rarely* (can, cannot) be moved to any of the positions marked by the slanted line.
	☐ Show with a slanted line where the adverb *slowly* can appear in this sentence.
/The car/drove/ around the corner/.	*The car drove around the corner.*

REVIEW

	Underline the adverbs in the following sentences.
<u>Recently</u> <u>badly</u>	☐ *Recently he has behaved badly.*
<u>rapidly</u> <u>sickeningly</u>	☐ *The car rapidly approaching the intersection skidded sickeningly.*
<u>conscientiously</u> <u>accurately</u>	☐ *The store manager conscientiously reported his income accurately.*

UNIT 3   CHOOSING ADJECTIVES AND ADVERBS

	Complete these sentences.
really	*We heard that the Masque Club put on a [real, really] fine show.*
well	*I answered the questions as [good, well] as I was able in those circumstances.*

□　　*The late edition of the paper arrived late.*

adjective

edition

adverb

arrived

The first *late* in this sentence is an (adjective, adverb) because it describes the noun _____. The second *late* is an (adjective, adverb) because it expresses *when* in regard to the verb _____.

□　　*A fast miler normally runs the quarter-mile fast.*

miler

how

Fast is an adjective in its first use because it describes the noun _____. This same word is an adverb in its second use because it expresses _____ in regard to the verb *runs*.

□ Modifiers such as *fast* and *late* have the same form whether they are adjectives or adverbs. Most adverbs, however, are distinguished from adjectives by an *ly* ending.

The attractive gift was wrapped attractively.

attractively

attractive

The adverb _____ in this sentence is the adjective _____ with *ly* added.

□ Notice the effect of adding *ly* to an adjective.

The attractive gift was wrapped attractively.

gift

how

The adjective *attractive* describes the noun _____; the adverb *attractively* expresses _____ the gift was wrapped.

□ While some modifiers do not have distinctive forms for their use as adjectives or adverbs, we form most of our adverbs by adding *ly* to adjectives. The adverb form of *fast* is _____. But the adverb form of *pure* is _____.

fast

purely

□ Certain adjectives are formed from nouns by the addition of *ly*. *Lovely* is formed from the noun *love,* and *manly* from the noun _____.

man

□ Generally speaking, a word with an added *ly* is an adjective if formed from a noun and an _____ if formed from an adjective.

adverb

134

□ If a modifier has two forms such as *happy* and *happily*, we use the adjective form to modify a noun or pronoun. Otherwise, we use the adverb form.

   We drove [bad, badly].

badly

Since the modifier in this sentence expresses *how* in regard to the verb *drove*, the adverb form, _____, is correct.

□ If in doubt about which word an adjective or adverb modifies, mentally omit the modifier to see which word is affected.

   The stream ran [rapid, rapidly] when it reached the bottom of the canyon.

ran   rapidly

Omitting the modifier here affects the meaning of (*stream, ran*). The correct form is _____.

□ Complete these sentences.

quietly
quiet

   We will spend the rest of the day [quiet, quietly].
   We look forward to a [quiet, quietly] day.

□ *Good* is an adjective; *well* is an adverb.

   I did [good, well] on the exam.

did   well

The modifier in this sentence affects the meaning of *[I, did]*. The correct completion, therefore, is _____.

□ Decide which word the modifier affects before completing this sentence.

well

   The choir didn't sing very [good, well] today.

□ *Well* is an adjective only when it means healthy.

   A [good, well] child is a blessing.

well
good

If this sentence refers to a child in good health, the correct adjective is _____. If it refers to a well-behaved child, the correct adjective is _____.

□ Complete these sentences.

well	*Only [good, well] patients are released from this hospital.*
well	*Paul didn't do very [good, well] in physics last semester.*

REVIEW

Correct the following sentences where necessary. Mark correct sentences C.

quickly	
~~quick~~	□ *Get well quick!*
well	
~~good~~	□ *He planted the new grass really good.*
C	□ *The children behaved badly today.*
easily	
~~easy~~	□ *Charlie took the last hurdle easy in stride.*

UNIT 4   CHOOSING COMPARATIVE AND SUPERLATIVE MODIFIERS

	Saying that Dave is brighter than Bob is saying only that he is not the least bright person in the class.
	The above sentence contains the comparative adjective
brighter	_____ and the superlative adjective _____
least bright	_____.

□ Adjectives and adverbs modify by expressing some quality or characteristic of persons, things, or actions.

   Ralph is strong.

The adjective *strong* expresses a quality of the person

Ralph	named by the noun _____.

□ Modifiers can express more or most of a quality.

   Ralph is stronger than Ed.
   Ralph is the strongest member of the team.

stronger	The adjective _____ expresses more of the
strongest	quality of strength; the adjective _____
	expresses most of the quality.

136

most	☐ There are three ways in which a modifier can attribute a quality. It can express the quality in itself (*strong*), more of the quality (*stronger*), or _____ of the quality (*strongest*).
est	☐ The form of the modifier indicates the degree of a quality. For instance, the *er* ending of *stronger* indicates more of the quality. The _____ ending of *strongest* indicates most of the quality.
	☐ Modifiers attributing more or most of a quality are used in comparisons. *Ralph is stronger than Ed.*
more	The key word in this comparison is the adjective *stronger*. We know from its form that Ralph has (more, most) of the quality of strength when compared to Ed.
	☐ Adjectives attributing more of a quality to one person or thing in comparison to another are comparative adjectives. *Ralph is stronger than Ed.*
comparative	*Stronger* is a _____ adjective.
	☐ Adjectives attributing most of a quality to one person or thing in comparison to two or more others are superlative adjectives. Complete this sentence with the superlative adjective based on *strong*.
strongest	*Ralph is the _____ member of the team.*
greater *greatest*	☐ The ending *er* makes an adjective comparative; the ending *est* makes it superlative. The comparative form of *great* is _____; the superlative form is _____.
comparative superlative	☐ *Easier* is a _____ adjective, and *easiest* is a _____ adjective.

□ Generally, if an adjective has more than two syllables, we do not use the *er* and *est* endings to form the comparative and superlative. Instead, we use *more* with the adjective to form the comparative and *most* with the adjective to form the superlative. Thus, the comparative form of the four-syllable adjective *intelligent* is *more intelligent;* the superlative form is _____ *intelligent.*

most

□ We form the comparative adjective in one of two ways.

He is _____ than I.

The comparative form of *sad* to complete this sentence is _____. The comparative form of *miserable* is _____.

sadder
more miserable

□ *He is the _____ man I know.*

The superlative form of *happy* to complete this sentence is _____. The superlative form of *charitable* is _____.

happiest
most charitable

□ Adverbs, too, have comparative and superlative forms. Normally, one-syllable adverbs have a comparative form ending in *er* and a superlative form ending in *est*. The comparative form of the one-syllable adverb *fast*, then, is _____; the superlative form is _____.

faster   *fastest*

□ Most adverbs with two or more syllables end in *ly*. The comparative and superlative forms of these are made by adding them to *more* and *most*. Thus the comparative form of *easily* is _____ *easily;* the superlative form is _____ *easily.*

more
most

□ Any adjective or adverb ending in *er* or preceded by *more* is _____; any ending in *est* or preceded by *most* is _____.

comparative
superlative

□ *Brightest* is a _____ adjective. *More brightly* is a _____ adverb.

superlative
comparative

138

☐ Adjectives and adverbs have, in addition, a comparative form expressing less of a quality and a superlative form expressing least of a quality.

> *This house is less expensive than the other; it may be the least expensive house on this street.*

comparative
superlative

Less expensive is (comparative, superlative); *least expensive* is (comparative, superlative).

☐ Joining *less* to any modifier makes it comparative; joining *least* to it makes it superlative. Thus the comparative of *simple*, attributing less of that quality, is _____; the superlative of the same word, attributing least of that quality, is _____.

less simple

least simple

☐ We recognize as comparative any adjective or adverb ending in *er* or preceded by *more* or _____.

less

☐ We recognize as superlative any adjective or adverb ending in *est* or preceded by _____ or _____.

most
least

☐ English has a few modifiers with irregularly formed comparatives and superlatives. The adjective *good*, for instance, has the comparative *better* and the superlative *best*. Complete these sentences with the correct form of *good*.

better
best

> *This is a _____ movie than that.*
> *This is the _____ movie we have seen.*

☐ The adverb *well* has comparative and superlative forms identical to those of the adjective *good*. Complete these sentences with the appropriate forms of *well*.

better
best

> *Harris writes _____ than I do.*
> *Of the three of us, Harris writes _____.*

	☐ The adjective *bad* and the adverb *badly* have identical comparative and superlative forms. The comparative of both is *worse*; the superlative is *worst*.
	She is a worse student than he. *She acts worse than you.*
comparative	*Worse* in the first sentence is the comparative of the adjective *bad*. This same modifier in the second sentence is the _____ of the adverb *badly*.
superlative	☐ Whether it is regularly or irregularly formed, a modifier is comparative if it attributes more or less of a quality; it is (comparative, superlative) if it attributes most or least.
	☐ *He is the least awkward of the dancers.* *He is a better dancer than his partner.*
superlative comparative	*Least awkward* in the first sentence is a (comparative, superlative) adjective; *better* in the second sentence is a (comparative, superlative) adjective.

more happily
~~*happier*~~
easily
~~*easiest*~~
	Replace any incorrect word in the following sentences with the correct form.
	
	    The men seem to work happier under the new manager than they did under the former one.
	    These men are the least easiest pleased of any I know.

	☐ Comparative and superlative adjectives, like other adjectives, modify nouns or pronouns.
	He is quicker than I.
He	The comparative modifier *quicker* in this sentence is an adjective attributing more of the quality of quickness to a person named by the pronoun _____.
	☐ Comparative and superlative adverbs modify verbs.
	He thinks more quickly than I.
thinks	The comparative modifier *more quickly* is an adverb attributing more of the quality of quickness to an action expressed by the verb _____.

140

□ Since many comparative and superlative modifiers are identical in form whether adjectives or adverbs, use determines what they are.

> *Ben tries harder than Ned.*
> *Ned has a harder time than Ben.*

adverb

adjective

Harder in the first sentence is a comparative (adjective, adverb) because it attributes the quality to the action of trying. In the second sentence it is a comparative (adjective, adverb) because it attributes the quality to a thing, time.

□ Choosing modifiers that have the same form for use as either adjective or adverb involves no difficulty. *Hard* is one such modifier; *high* is another.

> *This car has a higher roof than that.*
> *This flag should be raised higher than that.*

adjective
adverb

We know from its use that *higher* is an (adjective, adverb) in the first sentence and an (adjective, adverb) in the second.

□
> *This car has a higher roof than that.*
> *This flag should be raised higher than that.*

a thing

an action

Higher is an adjective in the first sentence because it attributes the quality to (a thing, an action). It is an adverb in the second sentence because it attributes the quality to (a thing, an action).

□ Many comparative and superlative modifiers, however, are adjectives or adverbs according to their form. *Happier* is a

comparative

comparative adjective; *more happily* is a _____ adverb.

adjective
adverb

□ *Easiest* is a superlative (adjective, adverb); *most easily* is a superlative (adjective, adverb).

141

□ If a comparative or superlative modifier has separate adjective and adverb forms, our choice depends on whether the quality expressed by the modifier is attributed to a person or thing or to an action.

> *This package is the [most attractive, most attractively] one we have.*
> *This package is the [most attractive, most attractively] wrapped of all.*

Since the modifier in the first sentence attributes the quality to a thing, the correct form is _____

most attractive

_____. Since the modifier in the second sentence attributes the quality to an action, the correct form

most attractively

is _____.

□ Complete these sentences, basing your choice of modifier on whether a person or thing or an action is modified.

steadier

> *I have a [steadier, more steadily] hand now than I used to.*

more steadily

> *I am pleased that I can work [steadier, more steadily] now than I used to.*

□ Complete these sentences.

less forceful
less forcefully

> *Charlie is [less forceful, less forcefully] than his father.*
> *Charlie speaks [less forceful, less forcefully] than his father.*

Replace any incorrect word in the following sentences with the correct form.

greater
~~greatest~~
least
~~less~~

> *When we compare the two stock issues, we see that the first has the greatest real value.*
> *Left to his own devices, John would buy the stock on this list of ten which had the less value.*

142

□ We use a comparative modifier only when comparing one person, thing, or action to one other.

> *Your date is prettier than mine.*

Since this is a comparison of one person with one other, the (comparative, superlative) adjective *prettier* is correct.

comparative

□ A comparison of one person, thing, or action with two or more others requires a superlative modifier.

> *Of the eight men in the department, Jones is the [worse, worst] choice for promotion.*

Since this is a comparison of one man to several others, the correct modifier is _____, the (comparative, superlative) form.

worst
superlative

□ *Which brand of cola is [stronger, strongest]?*

If we are comparing three or more brands of cola, we will complete this sentence with _____. If we are comparing only two, we will complete the sentence with _____.

strongest

stronger

□ Most sentences clearly require either the comparative or the superlative modifier. Select the correct modifier for each of these.

> *Of our two starting tackles, Bob is the [heavier, heaviest].*
> *Of our three starting quarterbacks, Jim is the [better, best] passer.*

heavier

best

□ Cross out the incorrect modifier and replace it with the correct one.

> *Which is the larger city, Cleveland, Omaha, or Dallas?*
> *Which color do you like best, red or white?*

largest
~~larger~~
better
~~best~~

Correct the following sentences where necessary. Mark correct sentences C.

C

☐ *Mr. Jones is the more talkative of the two teachers.*

efficiently
~~efficient~~

☐ *I am able to work more efficient now that my office is air-conditioned.*

fastest
~~faster~~
prettier
~~prettiest~~

☐ *Of the four cars entered in the first race, Rosell's is the faster.*

☐ *Which model has the prettiest hair, Jane or Ellen?*

more easily
~~easier~~

☐ *The power mower will allow you to mow your lawn easier than the conventional type.*

UNIT 5   CHOOSING ADJECTIVES AS SUBJECTIVE COMPLEMENTS

Complete these sentences.

bad

The judge felt [bad, badly] about the young criminal's sentence.

worthy

The judge proved [worthy, worthily] in his appointed position

☐ Choosing the correct form of a modifier to follow a verb will be difficult if we do not know what it modifies.

Henry behaved foolishly.
Henry was foolish.

Foolishly in the first sentence is an adverb modifying the action verb *behaved*. *Foolish* in the second sentence is an adjective modifying the subject, the noun _____.

Henry

□ A linking verb joins an adjective to the subject which it modifies.

> *Henry was foolish.*

was

foolish

In this sentence the linking verb _____ joins the adjective _____ to the subject it modifies, *Henry.*

□ Linking verbs plus their adjective complements express a state of being rather than an action of the subject.

> *She looks happy.*

a state of being

Happy, the adjective modifying the subject *She,* is joined to the subject by the linking verb *looks.* Together, the verb and the adjective express (an action, a state of being) of the subject.

□ English has four kinds of linking verbs which, together with an adjective as complement, can express a state of being rather than an action of the subject.

> Being: *be, remain, stay, keep, prove*
> Becoming: *become, get, turn, grow*
> Seeming: *seem, look, appear, act*
> Sensing: *feel, taste, smell, sound*

adjective

All of these verbs have this in common: they can link an (adjective, adverb) to the subject which it modifies.

□ 　*Yesterday I felt [bad, badly].*

Since *felt* expresses a state of being rather than an action of the subject, the correct modifier is the adjective

bad

_____.

□ Many verbs such as *feel* can express either an action or a state of being of the subject. Only if a verb expresses a state of being do we use an adjective as its complement. Choose completions for these sentences.

awkward

> *Mr. Smith felt [awkward, awkwardly] in front of the large audience.*

awkwardly

> *Mr. Smith felt [awkward, awkwardly] through his pockets in search of his notes.*

☐ When choosing a modifier to follow a verb, determine whether the verb expresses an action or a state of being of the subject.

suddenly
sudden

> *The truck appeared [sudden, suddenly].*
> *His action appeared [sudden, suddenly].*

☐ Complete these sentences, keeping in mind that *good* is always an adjective and that *well* is an adverb unless it means in good health.

good
well

> *Bob felt [good, well] in his tuxedo.*
> *Bob felt [good, well] after a few days in the hospital.*

☐ *Prove* is another verb that can link an adjective to the subject, but only if it expresses a state of being of the subject rather than an action. Complete these sentences.

ably
able

> *The lawyer proved his case [able, ably].*
> *The lawyer proved [able, ably] in presenting his case.*

☐ Always determine whether a verb expresses an action or a state of being of the subject before choosing a modifier to follow it.

silent

> *The prisoner remained [silent, silently] throughout the questioning.*

worthless

> *In all, over half of the corn crop looked [worthless, worthlessly].*

REVIEW

Correct the following sentences where necessary. Mark correct sentences C.

C
bad
~~badly~~

☐ *I really felt bad about his losing the match.*

☐ *The weather turned badly almost as soon as we left.*

good
~~well~~
uneasily
~~uneasy~~

☐ *My speakers sound well now that I have installed them in a new enclosure.*

☐ *Bob felt uneasy around the wall for the light switch.*

CHAPTER VIII

ILLOGICAL AND INCOMPLETE CONSTRUCTIONS

	UNIT 1 AVOIDING FAULTY SUBJECT-PREDICATE COMBINATIONS
The price of a Rolls Royce is relatively high. or *A Rolls Royce is relatively expensive.*	*The price of a Rolls Royce is relatively expensive.* Rewrite this sentence to clarify the logical relationship of its parts. _____ _____
Al	☐ The most important relationship in any sentence is that between the subject and the predicate. If the predicate is not a logical assertion about the subject, a sentence will be ambiguous. *Al's height is six feet tall.* The predicate *is six feet tall* is illogical because it is not Al's height but _____ who is six feet tall.
tall	☐ *Al's height is six feet tall.* We can make this sentence logical easily—by omitting one word, _____.

cost	☐ *The cost of living nowadays is extremely expensive.* This sentence is illogical because *is extremely expensive* cannot be asserted about the subject, the noun _____.
	☐ *The cost of living nowadays is extremely expensive.* Costs logically are not expensive but high. Complete the revision of this sentence.
is extremely high	*The cost of living nowadays* _____ _____ .
	☐ *My opinion of the movie is abominable.*
movie	This sentence is illogical because it is not the opinion but the _____ that the writer feels is abominable.
	☐ *My opinion of the movie is abominable.* The predicate *is abominable* will be logical only if the subject of the sentence is *movie*.
the movie is *abominable*	*In my opinion,* _____ .
Mr. Elkins	☐ *Mr. Elkins' job is a teacher.* This sentence is illogical because it is not the job but _____ who is a teacher.
Mr. Elkins	☐ *Mr. Elkins' job is a teacher.* Rewrite this sentence logically. _____ *is a teacher.*
	☐ *That phone call late last night was Rudy.* A phone call cannot be a person but rather from a person:
was from Rudy	*That phone call late last night* _____ _____ .

Rewrite any illogical sentence in the following group. Mark any sentence not needing revision C.

☐ *Before becoming political editor for the* Examiner, *Harold Rapke's profession was an economics teacher at Arizona State University.*

. . . *Harold Rapke was an economics teacher*

_____

_____

☐ *That wild cheering that broke out during the candidate's speech was the California delegation.*

. . . *was from the California delegation.*

_____

_____

☐ *The choice of the name for our boat was selected by my sister.*

. . . *was made by my sister*

or

The name for our boat was selected . . .

_____

_____

UNIT 2   AVOIDING ILLOGICAL COMPARISONS

Replace any incorrect word in this sentence.

ape's

~~ape~~

When he climbs the rope, Hal's arms seem as powerful as an ape.

☐ Expressing comparisons requires care to ensure that the persons or things compared are logically related.

Ralph is a better student than Pete.

This sentence is logical because it compares the abilities

Ralph   Pete

of two persons, _____ and _____.

☐ *Ralph's scholastic record is better than Pete.*

This sentence is not logical because it compares a thing, a

Pete

scholastic record, with a person, _____.

149

□   *Ralph's scholastic record is better than Pete.*

This sentence would be logical if it compared Ralph's scholastic record with _____ scholastic record.

Pete's

□   *Ralph's scholastic record is better than Pete's.*

This comparison is logical. Although *scholastic record* is not understood to follow *Pete* in the previous sentence, it is understood to follow the possessive form of that noun used in this sentence, _____.

Pete's

□   *Her skin is as smooth as a child.*

This comparison is illogical because it compares a thing, _____, with a person, _____.

skin   child

□   *Her skin is as smooth as a child.*
        Her skin is as smooth as a child's.

Although *skin* is not expressed twice, it can be understood to follow the final word only in the (first, second) sentence.

second

□   *Some have said that a newspaper reporter's responsibilities are graver than a doctor.*

Correct this comparison.

     Some have said that a newspaperman's responsibilities are graver _____.

than a doctor's

□   *The shape of the football used in the early days of the sport is different from the football now used.*

The error in this comparison is fairly well concealed. However, the sentence is illogical because it compares two unlike things, the _____ of the football formerly used and the _____ now used.

shape
football

□   Add the words necessary to make the comparison in the last frame logical.

     The shape of the football used in the early days of the sport is different from the _____ *football now used.*

shape of the

150

☐ *The shape of the football used in the early days of the sport is different from the shape of the football now used.*

If we wish to avoid repeating *the shape*, we can substitute the pronoun *that* for it in its second appearance:

that of the

The shape of the football used in the early days of the sport is different from _____ *football now used.*

☐ *The ship traffic on the Great Lakes is equivalent to any large American harbor.*

Correct this comparison, using the pronoun *that*.

to that in

The ship traffic on the Great Lakes is equivalent _____ _____ *any large American harbor.*

☐ *The plot of this play is far less complex than the novel upon which it is based.*

Correct this comparison.

than that of

The plot of this play is far less complex _____ _____ *the novel upon which it is based.*

REVIEW

Correct the following sentences by adding words where necessary. Mark correct sentences C.

those on or *hem-lines on* should be added after *than*.

☐ *Hemlines on women's dresses and skirts are a good deal higher now than the dresses and skirts worn by women in the last century.*

C

☐ *He is as fast as Charlie in the 10,000-meter run.*

that of or *the circu-lation of* is needed after *as large as*.

☐ *The publishers expect the circulation of the new* Life *magazine to be as large as the old* Life.

UNIT 3 PRONOUNS IN COMPARISONS

The coach expected more from Bob than [he, him].

If this sentence means that two people expected something of Bob, the coach and the person referred to by the pronoun, the correct pronoun is _____. If it means that the coach expected more from Bob than from the other person, the correct pronoun is _____.

he

him

☐ A pronoun following *as* or *than* is part of a comparison.

He is as tall as she.

This sentence compares the height of two persons referred to by the pronouns _____ and _____.

He   she

☐ A pronoun following *as* or *than* in a comparison is part of a subordinate clause often not fully expressed.

He is as tall as she [is tall].

Normally we would not express the words in the brackets. However, expressing them shows clearly that the pronoun *she* is the (subject, object) of the clause *as she [is tall].*

subject

☐ We do not fully express clauses following *as* or *than* because they would be unnecessarily repetitious.

Earl needs more time than she needs.

Ordinarily we would not express the verb _____ in the subordinate clause *than she needs* because it repeats the verb expressed in the main clause preceding it.

needs

☐   *She gave me more than she gave him.*

The meaning of this sentence would be as clear without the subordinate clause's subject and verb, _____, which are identical to those in the main clause.

she gave

152

☐   *Bob is less happy about it than she.*

is happy

The subordinate clause *than she* lacks two words, unexpressed because they are repetitious: _____.

☐   *It takes me longer than him.*

it takes

The subordinate clause *than him* lacks two unexpressed words which would precede *him*, _____.

☐ A pronoun following *as* or *than* in a comparison is subjective or objective depending on whether it is the subject or an object of a subordinate clause. Keep in mind that the clause may not be fully expressed.

   She is as fat as I.

subject

The subjective pronoun *I* is correct because the pronoun is the (subject, direct object) of the subordinate clause *as I [am fat].*

☐   *Tennis exhausts me as much as him.*

tennis [it] exhausts

Because *him* is the direct object of the subordinate clause *as [_____]* *him*, the objective pronoun used here is correct.

☐ If in doubt about which form of a pronoun to use following *as* or *than* in a comparison, supply the unexpressed parts of the clause to which it belongs.

   Pete is less clever than [I, me].

I am clever
subject
I

The complete subordinate clause here would be *than _____*. Since the pronoun is its (subject, direct object), the correct form is _____.

☐ Complete these sentences.

they
him

   The Smiths are as rich as [they, them].
   The odds are as much against Jack as [he, him].

□ The case of a pronoun following *as* or *than* in a comparison often indicates the meaning of the sentence.

> *Mary asked Hal more questions than [he, him].*

he asked Hal

If the subjective pronoun *he* is used, the subordinate clause completely expressed will be *than* _____.

□   *Mary asked Hal more questions than [he, him].*

On the other hand, if the objective pronoun *him* is used,

she asked him

the complete subordinate clause would be *than* _____ _____.

□   *Mary asked Hal more questions than he.*
       Mary asked Hal more questions than him.

first

These sentences have quite different meanings, indicated by the case of the pronoun following *than*. The (first, second) sentence indicates two questioners, Mary and the

second

person referred to by the pronoun. The (first, second) sentence indicates that two were questioned, Hal and the person indicated by the pronoun.

□   *I revere General Marshall as much as [he, him].*

If the meaning here is that General Marshall and someone else are revered, the subordinate clause completely ex-

I revere him
direct object
revere
him

pressed would be _____. The pronoun would, therefore, be the (subject, direct object) of the verb _____, and the correct pronoun would be _____.

□ Be sure that the case of the pronoun following *as* or *than* is correct according to the meaning of the sentence.

> *Senator Bruce pays more attention to his career than [she, her].*

her

If this sentence means that the Senator pays more attention to his career than to the person referred to by the pronoun, the correct pronoun is _____. If it means that he pays more attention to his career than does the person referred to by the pronoun, the correct pro-

she

noun is _____.

154

Correct the following sentences where necessary. Mark correct sentences C.

he
~~*him*~~

☐ *Hughes is considerably taller than him.*

C

☐ *I am as unhappy as she.*

she
~~*her*~~

☐ *I need far less help in math than her.*

he
~~*him*~~

☐ *Dr. Rogers expended far more energy on the assignment than him.*

UNIT 4   AVOIDING INCOMPLETE CONSTRUCTIONS

Add *I was* after *While.*

Correct this sentence by adding necessary words.

While sleeping off yesterday's exertions, the alarm clock rang noisily just out of my reach.

☐ To avoid unnecessary repetition, we often omit parts of subordinate clauses.

> *While I was studying, I ate two candy bars.*
> *While studying, I ate two candy bars.*

does not

The second sentence shows that omitting *I was* from the subordinate clause *While I was studying* in the first sentence (does, does not) make the sentence less clear.

☐ Clauses with parts missing but clearly understood are called elliptical clauses.

> *When traveling in London, Ellen lost her luggage.*

she [Ellen]

The words missing but clearly understood in the elliptical clause *When traveling in London* are _____ *was.*

155

□ *While he was campaigning, Nevins gave more than thirty speeches.*

The subordinate clause in this sentence will be just as clear if it is elliptical:

campaigning

While _____, Nevins gave more than thirty speeches.

□ The words omitted from an elliptical clause introducing a sentence are clearly understood only if the subject of the clause is the same as the subject of the sentence.

While he was working for the Rand Company, Cargill received a bonus every Christmas.

refer

The words *he was* can be omitted from the introductory clause in this sentence because *he* and *Cargill* (refer, do not refer) to the same person.

□ Using an elliptical clause whose omitted subject is different from the subject of the sentence makes a sentence confusing.

While bathing, the doorbell rang twice.

Since we expect the subject of an elliptical clause to refer to the same person or thing as the subject of the sentence, this sentence seems to suggest that the

doorbell

_____ was bathing.

□ To avoid confusing your reader even momentarily, supply the missing parts of elliptical clauses whose omitted subjects are different from the subjects of their sentences. Rewrite the sentence in the last frame, using *Carol* as the subject of the clause.

Carol was

While _____ bathing, the doorbell rang twice.

□ *When opening the can, Bob spilled its contents on the floor.*
When opening the can, the contents spilled on the floor.

second

The elliptical clause only in the (first, second) sentence requires the missing words *Bob was.*

156

☐   *When opening the can, the contents spilled on the floor.*

Correct the error in this sentence, giving the elliptical clause the subject *Bob.*

When Bob was open-ing the can

_____,

the contents spilled on the floor.

☐   *When ten years old, my father moved our family to California.*

Correct this sentence, supplying the elliptical clause with the logical subject.

When I was ten years old

_____,

my father moved our family to California.

☐ Correct this sentence.

    When running for the bus, a car almost hit me.

When I was run-ning for the bus

_____,

a car almost hit me.

    The French are far more interested in attracting tourists to their country than Americans.

are
Americans

This sentence will make sense only if _____ is added after _____.

☐ We often omit words from comparisons in order to avoid unnecessary repetition.

    This gear turns faster than that wheel turns.

is not

Repeating *turns* after *wheel* (is, is not) necessary.

☐   *Ralph runs the quarter-mile as fast as Bob runs the quarter-mile.*

will

If we remove *runs the quarter-mile* repeated after *Bob,* this sentence (will, will not) be just as clear.

☐ Cross out the words unnecessarily repeated in this sentence.

Some say that radio provides better news coverage than television provides.

. . . television provides

☐ We can omit from comparisons those words which are clearly understood.

Water boils at a lower temperature in higher altitudes than at sea level.

The omitted words clearly understood after *than* are

_____.

[water] it boils

☐ Omitting words from comparisons without causing ambiguity is possible only if the missing words are clearly understood.

Mr. Blake offered me more money than John.

This comparison is ambiguous because we do not know which words are missing. Either *he gave* is missing after *than* or *gave me*—or simply *did*—is missing after _____.

John

☐ If words omitted from a comparison are not clearly understood, we should supply them.

Dan helps Peter more often than Art.

If this sentence means that Dan helps both Peter and Art, we should add the words _____ between *than* and *Art*.

he helps

☐ *Dan helps Peter more often than Art.*

If this sentence means instead that Dan and Art both help Peter, we should add the two words _____ or the single word _____ after *Art*.

helps him
does

158

	☐ *Phillip is more concerned with business success than his family.*
	To make it clear that this sentence expresses a comparison between Phillip's concern and his family's concern, we
is	should add the word _____ after *family*.
	☐ *Phillip is more concerned with business success than his famil family.*
	If this comparison is instead between Phillip's concern for business success and his concern for his family, we
with	should add the preposition _____ before
his	_____.

REVIEW

In the following sentences, add any necessary words and cross out any unnecessary words. Mark correct sentences C.

	☐ *Before studying the problem, Baker was less able to see its complexities than Norton.*
C	
he was	☐ *While he was trying on the suit, John ripped open a seam on the coat.*
. . . *my class* ~~can~~ ~~write~~	☐ *I can write as well as anyone else in my class can write.*
I admire should be added before *Bob*; or *admires him*—or simply *does*—should be added after *Bob*.	☐ *I admire Hank much more than Bob.*

159

UNIT 5 MAINTAINING PARALLELISM

Strengthen the parallelism in this sentence by careful revision.

To maintain adequate security and at the same time allowing appropriate information to be made public are requirements which many governmental agencies have difficulty satisfying.

to allow
~~*allowing*~~

☐ The coordinating conjunctions such as *and, but,* and *or* join words and word groups of equal importance.

Milk and cheese are considered dairy products.

This sentence has a compound subject composed of two nouns equally important, _____ and _____.

Milk   cheese

☐   *He may go or stay.*

This sentence has a compound predicate composed of two verbs of equal importance, _____ and _____. They are joined by the coordinating conjunction _____.

go   stay
or

☐ We often use compound elements in our sentences to express two or more closely related ideas of equal importance. Normally, parts of a compound sentence element have the same grammatical form.

Milk and cheese are considered dairy products.
He may go or stay.

The compound subject of the first sentence and the compound predicate of the second sentence (have, do not have) the same grammatical form.

have

□ Parts of a compound sentence element having the same grammatical form are said to be parallel.

Missing a train and losing a sure bet are distressing experiences.

are

The parts of the compound subject in this sentence, the verbal phrases *Missing a train* and *losing a sure bet*, (are, are not) parallel.

□ Maintaining parallelism—that is, using the same grammatical form in compound sentence elements—is not an exercise in decorative symmetry. Rather, it stresses the equality of the ideas expressed.

The child plays happily and with vigor.

happily
with vigor

Here two ideas of equal importance joined by *and* lack parallelism. One part is an adverb, _____; the other is a prepositional phrase, _____.

□ *The child plays happily and with vigor.*

Although some might think that calling this sentence incorrect is undue faultfinding, this sentence will be smoother and the relationship between the modifiers clearer if we use a one-word adverb in place of *with vigor*.

vigorous

The child plays happily and _____ ly.

□ *Blond-haired and with blue eyes, Mary catches men's attention easily.*

Stressing the parallelism between the adjective and the prepositional phrase joined by *and* requires converting the phrase *with blue eyes* to a hyphenated modifier like *Blond-haired*.

eyed

Blond-haired and blue-_____, Mary catches men's attention easily.

☐ *His favorite recreations were making furniture and to sail his sloop.*

The breakdown in parallelism here is fairly obvious. *To sail* should be an *-ing* form rather than a *to* form to be parallel to *making*.

sailing

His favorite recreations were making furniture and _____ his sloop.

☐ *To be ready with a quip and having a fund of tall stories at hand were his secret ambitions.*

Correct the parallelism in this sentence.

to have

To be ready with a quip and _____ a fund of tall stories at hand were his secret ambitions.

☐ The correlatives such as *either . . . or, neither . . . nor,* and *not only . . . but also* join the parts of compound sentence elements.

Neither radio nor television provides the careful voter with adequate information.

Neither . . . nor

Two nouns, *radio* and *television,* are joined by the correlative _____.

☐ Parts joined by correlatives should be parallel.

Henry was not only a skilled physician but also ambitious.

Not only . . . but also joins the noun *physician* to the adjective *ambitious.* By rearranging the sentence parts slightly, we can put the adjectives *skilled* and *ambitious* in parallel positions.

skilled but also ambitious

Henry was a physician not only _____ _____.

	☐ *We spent those relaxed hours either strolling along the quiet streets or in the swimming pool.*
	Strengthen the parallelism in this sentence.
swimming in the pool	*We spent those relaxed hours either strolling along the quiet streets or _____.*
	☐ *His leg is neither healing nor much worse.*
	Neither . . . nor in this sentence joins a verb, *healing,* and an adjective, *worse.* Adding an appropriate verb after *nor* will strengthen the parallelism:
becoming [getting]	*His leg is neither healing nor _____ much worse.*
Add *on* before *the low hills* in the first sentence. Add *that* before *Mr. Harris* in the second.	Strengthen the parallelism in the following sentences. *Whether on the beach's gray sand cleared by the shifting tide or the low hills rolling eastward, the relics of D-Day are now few indeed.* *We respectfully request that Mr. Gunther be granted full power of attorney and Mr. Harris be named executor.*
	☐ Repeating a preposition in short parallel constructions is often unnecessary.
	He is in the kitchen or [in] the basement.
would not	Omitting the bracketed preposition *in* (would, would not) make this sentence less clear.
	☐ Repeating prepositions in longer parallel constructions stresses the parallelism and prevents misreading.
	He is on the beach sunning himself or the pier fishing.
or	We can stress the parallelism between the two nouns joined by *or, beach* and *pier,* by repeating the preposition *on* after _____.

163

□ *The government has made some effort to provide work for older people unemployed by technological advances and young people inadequately trained in the higher skills.*

The parallelism between the two parts of this sentence following *work* will be clearer if we repeat the preposition _____ after the word _____.

for   and

□ Add the preposition necessary to strengthen the parallelism in this sentence.

Add *beyond* after *and* or *even*.

   Bach's complex musical structures are beyond the comprehension of the casual listener—and even that of some serious students of music.

□ We often omit *whom, which,* and *that* introducing subordinate clauses in short parallel constructions.

   This is a record that Ralph likes and [that] I abhor.

Omitting the bracketed *that* from this sentence (would, would not) make it less clear.

would not

□ If parallel subordinate clauses are relatively long, it is wise to repeat *whom, which,* or *that* to introduce each clause.

   This is the record that Ralph likes more than any of the others he owns and [that] I abhor.

Here, repeating *that* following *and* (would, would not) help show the parallelism between the two subordinate clauses.

would

□ *The truck which broke down yesterday and had been repaired several times was scrapped.*

To stress the parallelism between the two subordinate clauses in this sentence, we should repeat _____ after _____.

which and

☐   *This is the pilot whom you perhaps remember meeting in London and you flew back to New York with.*

To stress the parallelism between the subordinate clauses in this sentence, we should repeat _____ after _____.

whom
and

☐ Add the word necessary to stress the parallelism between the subordinate clauses in this sentence.

Add *that* after *and.*

    I suggest that the committee find a remedy for our lack of funds and John Nevins be appointed the committee chairman.

☐ Add the word necessary to stress the parallelism in this sentence.

Add *that* after *or.*

    The persimmon trees that the harvesters injured with their trucks last autumn or the frost injured last winter will require special care.

REVIEW

Strengthen the parallelism in the following sentences where necessary. Mark any sentence not requiring changes C.

digging
~~to dig~~

☐   *The child seemed to prefer playing on the gym equipment and to dig in the sand pile.*

unsuccessfully
~~without success~~

☐   *In his efforts to make the varsity, John tried valiantly but without success.*

Add *that* after and.

☐   *This is the route that is best in bad weather and takes you through less mountainous terrain.*

what
~~the things~~

☐   *We are often known by what we say rather than the things we think.*

CHAPTER IX

PUNCTUATION AND CAPITALIZATION

UNIT 1 PUNCTUATING INTRODUCTORY ADVERBIALS

	Lately we have had other problems.
optional	A comma after *Lately* is (optional, necessary).

☐ Single adverbs introducing sentences are most often the free-floating kind that can be in other positions within the sentence.

Frantically he searched his pockets / for a dime / .

can   The adverb *Frantically* (can, cannot) appear in the other positions marked by the slanted lines.

☐ An introductory adverb that can appear in other positions does not require a comma to separate it from its sentence.

Sadly he walked away without the apple.

can   A comma after *Sadly* is not necessary because this adverb (can, cannot) appear in other positions within the sentence.

166

	☐ Occasionally writers use a comma to separate an introductory adverb from its sentence in order to emphasize it.
	Angrily the clerk stalked off.
Angrily	Only if he or she wished to emphasize the adverb would a writer place a comma after _____.
	☐ *Graciously Mr. Carr asked me in.*
is	This sentence (is, is not) correct as it stands.
	☐ Punctuate this sentence to stress the introductory adverb.
Graciously, Mr. Carr	*Graciously Mr. Carr asked me in.*
	☐ Sometimes a comma separating an introductory adverb from its sentence is necessary to prevent misreading.
	Typed copies have become available recently. *Recently typed copies have become available.*
is	If the second sentence is to have the same meaning as the first, a comma after *Recently* (is, is not) necessary.
	☐ Punctuate the second sentence to give it the same meaning as the first.
Rapidly, moving	*Moving clouds rapidly covered the blue sky.* *Rapidly moving clouds covered the blue sky.*
	☐ *Outside Mr. John felt better.* *Outside the house looked bleak.*
first second	A comma after *Outside* would be superfluous in the (first, second) sentence but necessary in the (first, second) sentence to prevent misreading.
	Add the necessary punctuation to the following sentences.
(b) However, by	(a) *However we decide to go, we should try to be there by morning.* (b) *However by taking Highway One, we will be able to see the scenery along the coast.*

□ A certain kind of introductory adverb called a conjunctive adverb normally requires a comma. *However, therefore, moreover, nevertheless,* and *consequently* are conjunctive adverbs we commonly use. Punctuate this sentence.

Moreover, he

Moreover he refuses to return.

□ As their name suggests, conjunctive adverbs have two functions. In addition to being adverbs, they join the idea expressed in their own sentence to an idea expressed in a previous sentence.

Our overall productivity this year was unusually low. Nevertheless, we expect our profits to be substantial.

Without the sentence preceding it, the conjunctive adverb *Nevertheless* (would, would not) be meaningless.

would

□ When we set them off with commas, we show that introductory conjunctive adverbs serve the dual function of modifying and connecting. Add the necessary comma to this sentence.

Moreover, this

Moreover this year's stock dividend will be higher than last year's.

□ We can see clearly the dual function of a conjunctive adverb if we move it to another position in a sentence.

This year's stock dividend, moreover, will be higher than last year's.

The pull which we feel *moreover* to have toward preceding ideas makes the word an interruption when it appears farther along in the sentence. Since we normally set off interruptions, commas before and after *moreover* (are, are not) necessary.

are

□ A comparison of the following sentences shows the difference between an introductory adverb and an introductory conjunctive adverb.

> *Suddenly he shouted to his teammates.*
> *However, he shouted to his teammates.*

The adverb *Suddenly* can be moved to follow *shouted* without becoming an interruption requiring commas, while *However* (can, cannot).

cannot

□ Add any comma necessary in these sentences.

> (a) *Finally we left.*
> (b) *Consequently we left.*

(b) *Consequently, we left*

□ *However* and *then* are two conjunctive adverbs which can function simply as adverbs. If *however* means *nevertheless*, it is a conjunctive adverb; if it means *no matter how*, it is an adverb.

> *However hard she tried, she could not finish.*
> *However, she could not finish.*

second

However is a conjunctive adverb in the (first, second) sentence and an adverb meaning *no matter how* in the (first, second) sentence.

first

□ Add any necessary comma to these sentences.

> (a) *However we do it, let's do it now.*
> (b) *However we should do it correctly.*

(b) *However, we*

□ When *then* means *consequently*, it is a conjunctive adverb. When it means *at that time*, it is an adverb.

> *You will, then, remember me in your will.*
> *You will remember then that I am your loving nephew.*

a conjunctive adverb

In the first sentence *then* is (a conjunctive adverb, an adverb); in the second sentence it is (a conjunctive adverb, an adverb).

an adverb

	☐ Add any necessary commas to these sentences. Remember that a conjunctive adverb appearing within a sentence is an interrupter requiring commas before and after it.
(a) *We have, then,*	(a) *We have then only four chairs.* (b) *We had only four chairs then.*
	☐ Add any comma necessary in these sentences.
	(a) *Do it however you wish.*
(b) *it, however, my*	(b) *Do it however my way.*

Add only necessary punctuation to these sentences.

(a) *On the assembly line we make car radios.*

(b) *On the whole, we*   (b) *On the whole we make a fine product.*

☐ We often introduce our sentences with word groups called prepositional phrases, made up of a preposition together with a noun and its related words: *to the beach, over the high walls, in the very beginning,* for instance. Introductory prepositional phrases are like adverbs. It is characteristic of them also that they can appear in other positions within their sentences.

At this time we cannot / hire you / .

can   The phrase *At this time* (can, cannot) be moved to either of the positions marked by the slanted lines.

☐ Since introductory prepositional phrases can be placed in any one of several positions in a sentence, they are not interrupters and do not need to be set off with commas.

In his work he is extremely conscientious.

is not   A comma following *work* (is, is not) necessary.

☐ Introductory prepositional phrases are often followed by others related to them. Normally, commas setting off such groups are unnecessary.

Before the date of the flood Noah built his ark.

is not   A comma following *flood* (is, is not) necessary.

170

☐ If an introductory prepositional phrase, together with its related phrases, is so long that it might obscure the beginning of the main clause, a comma should follow it to mark where the subject of the sentence begins.

> *In addition to barking dogs and screaming children we heard a passing fire truck blaring its siren.*

children

We should place a comma after _____.

☐ Add any comma necessary in the following sentences.

> (a) *After a while he began to enjoy his work immensely.*

(b) cannery, he

> (b) *After a long time on the night shift at the cannery he decided to quit.*

☐ Certain introductory prepositional phrases, like conjunctive adverbs, serve both as modifiers and as connectives. Such phrases are set off with commas for the same reason that conjunctive adverbs are.

> *Moreover, the rifle jammed.*
> *In addition, the rifle jammed.*

These examples show that, since it can replace the conjunctive adverb *Moreover*, the prepositional phrase

In addition

_____ serves as a connective as well as an adverb.

☐ *After all, for example, in addition, on the whole,* and *on the contrary* are a few of the introductory prepositional phrases that also function as connectives. We should normally set these off with commas from the sentences they introduce. Add the necessary comma to this sentence.

whole, he's

> *On the whole he's not very pleased with me.*

☐ Prepositional phrases which function as connectives as well as modifiers are set off by commas wherever they appear in a sentence.

> *He is, on the contrary, a fine instructor.*

are

The commas before and after *on the contrary* (are, are not) necessary.

171

☐ Add any necessary punctuation to these sentences.

(a) *whole, business*

    (a) *On the whole business is good.*
    (b) *On the left we can see Baja California.*

☐ Add any necessary punctuation to these sentences. Remember that a prepositional phrase that is also a connective should have a comma before and after it when it appears in the middle of its sentence.

    (a) *He made ten mistakes in addition and one in subtraction.*

(b) *made, in addition,*
        four

    (b) *He made in addition four mistakes in multiplication.*

☐ Add any comma necessary to these sentences.

(a) *cannot, after all,*
(b) *example, we*

    (a) *We cannot after all please everyone.*
    (b) *For example we cannot please him.*

REVIEW

Add the necessary punctuation to and remove unnecessary punctuation from the following sentences. Mark correct sentences C.

The comma is not
necessary.

☐ *In the beginning, he was fine.*

C

☐ *However you decide to do it, do it now.*

all, he's

☐ *After all he's only a baby.*

insist, moreover, that

☐ *The men insist moreover that their fringe benefits are inadequate.*

172

Add any necessary punctuation to the following sentences.

(a) *successfully, we*

(b) *pleasantly, he*

(a) *To fish successfully we need patience.*

(b) *Smiling pleasantly he hit me in the mouth.*

☐ Earlier in this text you learned that we can combine sentences having the same subject by joining the predicate of one sentence to the other.

> *He was smiling at our embarrassment. He left.*
> *Smiling at our embarrassment, he left.*

does

The second word group here (does, does not) have the same meaning as the first.

☐ The predicate of one sentence combined with another is called a verbal phrase. *Smiling at our embarrassment,* then,

verbal

is an example of a _____ phrase.

☐ Verbal phrases are so named because they are based on a form of a verb, often the *-ing* form.

> *Running hard, they caught the bus.*

Running hard

Here the verbal phrase is _____.

☐ Verbal phrases can also be based on the *to* form of the verb: *to fly, to swim, to become.*

> *He found the address. He asked a paperboy.*
> *To find the address, he asked a paperboy.*

The verbal phrase in the final sentence here is _____

To find the address

_____.

☐ Often we introduce sentences with a verbal phrase.

> *Remembering his manners, Henry apologized.*

Remembering his manners

This sentence is introduced by the verbal phrase _____

_____.

173

□ We should always place a comma after introductory verbal phrases. Add the necessary commas to these sentences.

(a) *Grinning happily, he*

(b) *auditorium, you*

  (a) *Grinning happily he left us standing there.*
  (b) *To be heard in the rear of the auditorium you must speak loudly.*

□ The reason we should always place a comma after introductory verbal phrases is that the separation between them and the main clause is often not clear without the comma. Punctuate this sentence.

certain, the

  To be certain the scientists checked their figures three times.

□ Add the comma necessary in this sentence.

questioning, the

  After questioning the prisoner was returned to his cell.

□ Add the comma necessary to make it clear that *Hughes* is not the subject of this sentence.

Hughes, the

  In appointing Hughes the supervisor blundered badly.

□ Add the necessary commas to these sentences.

(a) *answered, Jones*

(b) *health, you*

  (a) *Having answered Jones sat down.*
  (b) *To regain your health you will need rest.*

REVIEW

Add the necessary punctuation to the following sentences. Mark correct sentences C.

sure, Ralph

□ *To be sure Ralph decided to look for himself.*

yesterday, Bob

□ *Going to work yesterday Bob had a bad accident.*

C

□ *To allow yourself enough time, start by eight.*

speaking, revolutions

□ *Strictly speaking revolutions on college campuses are not new.*

174

Add any punctuation necessary to these sentences.

(a) *Well you can see now my friend that our troubles have just begun.*

(b) *No I can't.*

(a) *Well, you now, my friend, that*

(b) *No, I*

☐ Interjections are words that convey a feeling through sound. *Ouch* and *wow* are examples of strong interjections which we usually punctuate separately with exclamation marks. *Oh, well,* and *indeed* are mild interjections which we sometimes join to sentences.

> *Oh, I didn't know.*

interjection

This sentence is introduced by the _____ *Oh*.

☐ Since interjections derive their expressive force from their sound, they are characteristic of the spoken rather than the written language. Occasionally, however, we do use them in our writing. If quoting a speaker using a strong interjection, we punctuate it separately with an exclamation mark:

"Ouch!"

> *"Ouch"*

☐ A mild interjection used in a sentence is separated from the main clause by a comma. Punctuate this sentence.

Well, you

> *Well you can never tell.*

☐ Add the necessary punctuation to these sentences.

(a) *"Hey!"*
(b) *Indeed, I*

(a) *"Hey"*
(b) *Indeed I was amazed.*

175

☐ The words *yes* and *no* are a good deal like interjections, and we punctuate them the same way. Add the necessary punctuation to this sentence.

Yes, she

Yes she can go.

☐ Add the punctuation necessary in these sentences.

(a) Oh, is
(b) No, I

    (a) Oh is she really?
    (b) No I don't think so.

☐ Words of direct address in a sentence—*my friends, ladies and gentlemen, dear,* for instance—are always set off by commas.

    And now, ladies and gentlemen, let me tell you a really funny story.

are

The commas before and after *ladies and gentlemen* (are, are not) necessary.

☐ Add necessary commas to these sentences.

    (a) You are my friends of a lifetime.

(b) are, my friends,

    (b) You are my friends fine companions for a lifetime.

☐ Add any necessary punctuation to these sentences.

    (a) You are very dear.

(b) are, dear, a

    (b) You are dear a sight.

☐ In this same category are proper names of individuals we address. They also are normally set off with commas. Add the necessary comma here.

Mary, please

Mary please go to the store now.

☐ Remember to set off a word of direct address, including a proper name, with a comma before and after it if it interrupts a sentence. Add the necessary commas here.

know, Mr. Stevens, where

I don't know Mr. Stevens where your son is.

176

Add punctuation where necessary in the following sentences. Mark correct sentences C.

Indeed, it

☐ *Indeed it certainly is hot.*

going, George

☐ *Where are you going George?*

Yes, I

☐ *Yes I think he is here.*

UNIT 4   PUNCTUATING SERIES, DATES, AND ADDRESSES

Add the necessary punctuation to this sentence.

valley, climbed
hill, and

We hiked across the valley climbed the steep hill and descended to the town.

☐ Three or more words or phrases joined in a sentence are a series.

> *Paine lettered in football and basketball.*
> *Paine lettered in track, gymnastics, and swimming.*

the second

A series of nouns is illustrated by (the second, both) sentence(s).

☐ A series, although composed of three or more separate parts, normally has only one coordinating conjunction. A comma replaces conjunctions between the remaining parts of the series.

> *We grow apples and oranges and pears.*

Only in exceptional cases would we find the *and* after *apples* expressed as it is here. A comma usually replaces it:

, oranges and pears

> *We grow apples* _____.

177

□   *We grow apples, oranges and pears.*

Although this sentence is now adequately punctuated, most writers prefer to place another comma before *and* in sentences such as this to stress the division of the series' parts:

, and pears

    We grow apples, oranges _____ .

□ Punctuate this sentence, using a comma before the coordinating conjunction.

Babylon, Egypt, and

    These lectures will deal with the ancient civilizations of Babylon Egypt and India.

□ A sentence may contain a series composed of three or more phrases.

    We found him dashing around in circles waving his arms and shouting wildly.

three

This sentence has a series composed of (three, four) verbal phrases.

□ Phrases in series are punctuated in the same way that words in series are. Punctuate this sentence.

circles, waving
arms, and

    We found him dashing around in circles waving his arms and shouting wildly.

□ Subordinate clauses as well may be joined in series of three or more. Punctuate this sentence.

been, what
doing, and

    Mr. Blake asked Bob where he had been what he had been doing and why he was late.

□ If a compound sentence has three or more short independent clauses, we can punctuate them as a series:

door, Al
door, and

    I tried the front door Al tried the back door and Harry tried the window.

Add any necessary punctuation to the following sentences.

(a) *Japanese carrier planes bombed Pearl Harbor on Sunday December 7 1941.*

(b) *Please send your reply to William Burke 1517 Bay St. San Diego California.*

(a) Sunday, December 7, 1941

(b) William Burke, 1517 Bay St., San Diego, California

☐ Like punctuating a series, punctuating dates is simply a matter of separating the parts with commas.

She returned to this country on Tuesday, May 1, 1960.

This sentence (is, is not) correctly punctuated.

is

☐ Add the necessary punctuation to this sentence.

The Grant Hotel burned to the ground on Saturday August 14 1864.

Saturday, August 14, 1864

☐ We follow the same basic principle when only two of the three parts of a date are expressed:

This store will be closed after March 14 1963.

March 14, 1963

☐ If only one part of a date is expressed, it does not require punctuation.

I leave on June 11 for Madrid.

A comma (would, would not) be correct after *June 11.*

would not

☐ Add any necessary commas to these sentences.

(a) *I go to work on Monday August 7.*
(b) *His grandfather lived in Syracuse until July 4 1914.*

(a) Monday, August 7
(b) July 4, 1914

☐ Add any necessary commas to these sentences.

(a) *We moved in 1954 to Omaha.*
(b) *My brother Harry was born on Friday January 24 1946.*

(b) Friday, January 24, 1946

179

□ We use the same principles in punctuating addresses that we use in punctuating dates. An address may have as many as five parts—name, street address, city, state, and country. Add the necessary punctuation to this sentence.

Ralph Paul,
3411 Hazel St.,
Vancouver, British
Columbia, Canada

Ship this order to Ralph Paul 3411 Hazel St. Vancouver British Columbia Canada.

□ If only one part of an address is given, it does not require special punctuation.

We lived on Western Avenue until the war.

does not

This sentence (does, does not) require commas.

□ Two or more parts of an address require the same punctuation as two or more parts of a date. Add the necessary commas to this sentence.

Clint, Texas

He came all the way from Clint Texas.

□ Add any necessary commas to the following sentences.

(a) Russel Arne,
73 Novato Way,
Elko, Nevada

(a) *This letter is to be sent to Russel Arne 73 Novato Way Elko Nevada.*
(b) *Colorado is the right state, and 1163 is the right street number.*

REVIEW

Add punctuation where necessary in the following sentences. Mark correct sentences C.

Fresno, California

□ *The convention is to be held in Fresno California.*

dressing, Sue
cake, and

□ *Carol mixed the salad dressing Sue baked the cake and Dad poured the punch.*

C

□ *I returned in 1959 from the Eniwetok Proving Grounds to San Francisco.*

June, 1959
Syracuse, New York to
Hollister, California

□ *In June 1959 we moved from Syracuse New York to Hollister California.*

180

	He demanded only three things, health, wealth, and success.
	The comma after *things* should be replaced with a
colon dash	_____ or a _____.

☐ A series is any group of three or more words or phrases. We occasionally use a series as an appositive—that is, as an explanation of a particular word.

> *There are four cardinal virtues: prudence, justice, fortitude, and temperance.*

Here the appositive is a series since it contains **three or more words:** *prudence, justice, fortitude, and temperance.* It

virtues   explains the noun it follows, _____.

☐ An appositive which is not a series is normally set off with a comma.

> *He had only two shoes, a black oxford and a brown loafer.*

Here the appositive following *shoes* is set off by a comma because it enumerates only two things and is, **therefore,**

series   not a _____.

☐ An appositive which is a series should be set off with a colon (*:*) rather than a comma. Add the necessary colon to this sentence.

instruments: the

> *He plays three instruments the flute, the oboe, and the piano.*

☐ Don't mistake the colon for the semicolon, which has an entirely different use. The semicolon is formed by adding a dot over a comma (;), while the colon is formed by

dot   adding a dot over a _____.

□ The colon is an introducing mark, which is why we use it to introduce an appositive series.

> He plays three instruments: the flute, the oboe, and the piano.

If we substitute a comma for the colon, we can see why a comma would be incorrect following *instruments*.

> He plays three instruments, the flute, the oboe, and the piano.

Here *instruments* seems on first reading to be just another part of the series following it. That the three nouns of the series explain *instruments* (is, is not) clear.

is not

□ Although we cannot use a comma to introduce an appositive series, we can use a dash (—) in place of a colon. Place the dash in the appropriate place here.

instruments—the

> He plays three instruments the flute, the oboe, and the piano.

□ The difference between a colon and a dash introducing an appositive series is that a dash draws more attention to the series than a colon does.

> He brought three kinds of fruit apples, cherries, and peaches.

dash
colon

If we wish to focus attention on the series in this sentence, we will use a (dash, colon) following *fruit*. If not, we will use a (dash, colon).

□ Punctuate the appositive series in this sentence to focus attention on it.

Italy—Rome

> We visited three cities in Italy Rome, Venice, and Florence.

□ Punctuate the appositive series in this sentence in a way that does not focus attention on it.

friends: Walt

> He invited three friends Walt, Mac, and Leo.

182

	Correct the punctuation in this sentence.
courses—math *chemistry—because*	*This semester I'll be taking only three courses: math, physics, and chemistry because I have a part-time job.*

☐ Since a colon means *as follows,* we use it only if what comes between it and the end of the sentence is part of the enumeration or explanation it introduces.

> *I have three coins: a nickel, a dime, and a quarter.*
> *I will give you three coins: a nickel, a dime, and a quarter, to perform your trick.*

first
second

The colon is correct in the (first, second) sentence but not in the (first, second) sentence.

☐ If an appositive series comes within a sentence rather than at the end, we set it off with dashes—that is, we place a dash before and after the series. Punctuate the series in this sentence.

coins—a
quarter—to

> *I will give you three coins a nickel, a dime, and a quarter to perform your trick.*

☐

> *He owned three cars a Ford, a Chevrolet, and a Plymouth although he himself did not drive.*
> *He owned three cars a Ford, a Chevrolet, and a Plymouth.*

second
first

Although we can use either a colon or a dash after *cars* in the (first, second) sentence, we should use a dash both after *cars* and *Plymouth* in the (first, second) sentence.

☐ Add the necessary punctuation to these sentences, using dashes only where required.

(a) *tobacco—in*
cigars—its

(b) *usage: formal*

> (a) *Of the three ways of using tobacco in cigarettes, in pipes, and in cigars its use in cigarettes is by far the most dangerous.*
> (b) *Some scholars distinguish four levels of language usage formal, standard, colloquial, and substandard.*

183

Add punctuation needed in the following sentences, using a dash only where necessary. Mark correct sentences C.

aides —speech-writer

Long —before

☐ *Today the President-elect named three new aides speech-writer James Elder, foreign affairs adviser Ralph Briggs, and assistant press secretary Avery Long before departing for a short Christmas vacation.*

C

☐ *In homes today we use two important sources of power, natural gas and electricity.*

novels: A

☐ *I gave him a copy of each of Hemingway's early novels A Farewell to Arms, The Sun Also Rises, and To Have and Have Not.*

UNIT 6   USING COLONS AND DASHES TO EMPHASIZE APPOSITIVES

He had one dream, to live in Paris.
He had one dream, to live in Paris, and he finally realized it.

dash
colon
dashes

We can substitute either a _____ or a _____ for the comma in the first sentence. We can substitute only _____ for the commas in the second.

☐ Appositives following nouns are normally set off with commas.

My mother has only one prized possession, an antique clock.

is

Here the appositive *an antique clock,* which explains the noun *possession,* (is, is not) correctly punctuated with a comma.

☐ If we wish to emphasize an appositive that appears at the end of a sentence, we punctuate it with a colon. Place the colon in the appropriate place here.

possession: an

> *My mother has only one prized possession an antique clock.*

☐ We can also punctuate an appositive with a dash, giving it even more emphasis.

possession —an

> *My mother has only one prized possession an antique clock.*

☐   *Some employers insist that their employees have only one object security.*

comma
colon
dash

A _____ after *object* is the normal punctuation.
A _____ will emphasize the appositive *security;*
a _____ will emphasize *security* even more.

☐ If an appositive is not the last element in a sentence, we cannot use a colon. We must instead set it off either with commas or with dashes.

> *The company had a pact a working agreement with the union.*

We cannot use a colon after *pact.* we must use either

commas   dashes

_____ or _____ to set off *a working agreement.*

☐   *He had one disability a broken arm which kept him out of action.*
He had one disability a broken arm.

Depending upon the emphasis we want to give *a broken arm,* we will use either commas or dashes to set it off in

first
second

the (first, second) sentence. We can use a comma, a colon, or a dash after *disability* only in the (first, second) sentence.

Add to the following sentences the punctuation needed to give the appositive the kind of emphasis indicated.

☐ No emphasis:

fish, trout

    I like one kind of fish trout.

☐ Slight emphasis:

fish: trout

    I like one kind of fish trout.

☐ Strong emphasis:

fish —trout

    I like one kind of fish trout.

UNIT 7   USING COLONS TO INTRODUCE EXPLANATORY CLAUSES

Correct the punctuation in this sentence.

succession: the

    These events happened in quick succession; the car stopped, four men climbed out, and the car sped away.

☐ Occasionally we will join two closely related sentences with a semicolon to make them one sentence.

    The bank was not open; he was unable to cash the check.

Here two sentences—two independent clauses—are joined

semicolon   with a _____.

☐ Two or more independent clauses joined in one sentence form a compound sentence.

    The bank was not open; he was unable to cash the check.

is   This sentence (is, is not) a compound sentence.

□ Occasionally, however, the second independent clause in a compound sentence explains or amplifies the first.

> *The reason he gave was this: he had not been able to cash the check until the banks had opened.*

is

The second independent clause in this sentence (is, is not) an explanation of the first.

□ Since a colon means *as follows,* we use it rather than a semicolon after the first clause in a compound sentence if the clause or clauses following it are explanations or amplifications.

> *This much is certain: Henderson was there at the time and could have prevented the explosion.*

is

Since the second independent clause in this sentence is an amplification of the first, the colon (is, is not) correct.

□ We should never use a colon to separate clauses of a compound sentence unless the second clause explains or amplifies the first.

> *It was all too clear the box had in fact been opened.*
> *It was all too clear we needed little additional information.*

first
second

A colon should be placed after *clear* in the (first, second) sentence, a semicolon after *clear* in the (first, second) sentence.

□ Add a colon or a semicolon to these sentences.

(a) *most: he*

> (a) *Of all his fine traits, one impresses me most he never says an unkind word about anyone.*

(b) *most; his*

> (b) *Of all his fine traits, one impresses me most his others, however, are certainly worth mentioning.*

REVIEW

Add the punctuation necessary in the following sentences.

this: he

□ *His excuse was this he lost the slip of paper on which he had written the phone number.*

falls in	☐ *We planted the trees in the fall in the spring we planted additional bushes for a hedge.*
position: he	☐ *This was his position he would vote for the rules change if a majority of the other members favored it.*

UNIT 8   PUNCTUATING INTERRUPTERS

	Correct the punctuation in this sentence without rearranging its parts.
me—do why?—to	*"He asked me, do you know why?, to accompany him."*

☐ When speaking, we often interrupt a sentence in the middle to repeat an important point or to change the direction of our thought.

    "Will you please bring me—no, not that!"

The break in this sentence shows that some event or thought forced the speaker to stop one sentence abruptly and begin another. The punctuation marking the break is

dash

a _____.

☐ An abrupt shift in grammatical structure should be marked with a dash. Add the necessary dash to this sentence.

her—no

    "I'll ask her no, I can't."

☐ If an interruption comes in the middle of a sentence, we should place a dash before and after it to set it off:

am—rather
was—going

    "I am rather, I was going steady with her."

☐ Questions or exclamations which interrupt a sentence should be punctuated to show what they are and should be set off with dashes:

there—Ouch!—under

    "It hurts right there Ouch under my shoulder blade."

☐ Add the necessary punctuation to this sentence.

Hank—do
him?—who's

> *"There's Hank do you know him who's rich as Midas."*

☐ Although abrupt shifts and interruptions are characteristic of spoken rather than written expression, their occasional use for such specific purposes as emphasis and variety is the mark of mature prose. Add the dashes necessary in this sentence.

opportunity—the
opportunity—to

> *This is the last opportunity the absolutely last opportunity to offer a realistic plan.*

☐ Punctuate this sentence correctly.

paused—what
say?—and

> *The candidate paused what could he say and simply asked if there were any more questions.*

REVIEW

Add the necessary punctuation to the following sentences.

local—what
call it?—our

☐ *"And this is our local what do the students call it our local snake pit."*

excited—perhaps
accurate—when

☐ *She seemed excited perhaps hysterical is more accurate when she learned the good news.*

expensive—much
expensive—for

☐ *That car was expensive much too expensive for his budget.*

UNIT 9   USING PARENTHESES WITH INSERTED INFORMATION AND GUIDES

Correct the punctuation in the following sentences.

(a) chart (p. 14) in

(a) *Keep the chart, p. 14, in front of you as you read this chapter.*

(b) society: (1) an
car, (2) a
and (3) an

(b) *These are the three most powerful status symbols in our society: 1, an expensive car, 2, a large home, and 3, an important job.*

189

□ Parentheses (( )) are used primarily to set off information not essential in a sentence but interesting or helpful to some readers.

> *The illustration (p. 434) will help you understand the cost-profit relationship.*

Since the page number of the illustration mentioned is not important in this sentence but is added only as a help to the reader, it (is, is not) appropriately set off in parentheses.

is

□   *Tetanus lockjaw is still often fatal.*

Since *lockjaw* is added here to give the reader the common name for tetanus, we (should, should not) enclose *lockjaw* in parentheses.

should

□ Add the appropriate punctuation:

> *Tetanus lockjaw is still often fatal.*

(lockjaw)

□ Incidental information of all kinds should be set off in parentheses. For instance, if writing about the sugar maple tree, we may wish to include its Latin designation, *Acer saccharum,* to help a reader who is a botanist identify it according to the name with which he is familiar:

> *The sugar maple Acer saccharum is indigenous to the northeastern United States.*

(Acer saccharum)

□ Foreign words and phrases, which some readers may not understand, are appropriately translated in parentheses. Add parentheses here.

> *She said he was muy simpatico very nice.*

(very nice)

□ Add the necessary parentheses to these sentences.

    (a) *This quotation was taken from John Donne's sonnet "At the round earth's imagined corners" line 4.*
    (b) *Acrophobia fear of high places is a common neurosis often unrecognized by the sufferer.*

(a) (line 4)
(b) (fear of high places)

commas

(a) *(food poisoning)*

(b) *Botulism, a*
   foods, is

should

(a) *one*   (b) *a*
(c) *three* (d) *a*

☐ The indiscriminate use of parentheses to insert information at random is a mark of poor writing. Commas should generally be used if the information to be set off is related in any way to the sentence's main ideas.

> *Mr. Miller owner of Miller's Hardware will run for the city council.*

Although not essential to the sentence's meaning, the phrase *owner of Miller's Hardware* is related to the central idea of this sentence and should be set off with (commas, parentheses).

☐ Only one of the following sentences requires parentheses. Add the necessary punctuation to both.

> (a) *Botulism food poisoning has caused six deaths in the United States recently.*
> (b) *Botulism a bacillus often found in foods is extremely difficult to trace when large quantities of foods are involved.*

☐ Since parentheses show that added material does not belong to a sentence, we always use them to set off numbers used in enumerations.

> *In order to register properly, you must complete the following steps: (1) complete the forms provided, (2) have your adviser sign your study list, and (3) return all forms to the Registrar.*

To show that they do not belong to the sentence but are simply guides to reading, the numbers in this sentence (should, should not) be set off in parentheses.

☐ If letters instead of numbers are enumerating guides, we set them off in parentheses in the same way that we set off numbers. Add the parentheses to this sentence.

> *The clerk packed four items: a one dozen eggs, b a carton of milk, c three cans of apple juice, and d a large mousetrap.*

191

☐ When using numbers or letters in parentheses as guides in a series, we use commas in the same way that we would if the guides were not there. Add all the necessary punctuation to the following sentence.

(1) to answer the telephone, (2) to greet appointees, and (3) to type

A receptionist's duties are these: 1 to answer the telephone 2 to greet appointees and 3 to type occasional letters.

☐ Add all the necessary punctuation to this sentence.

(a) one shotgun, (b) twenty geese, and (c) an

The sheriff found the following items in the defendant's car: a one shotgun b twenty geese and c an out-of-date hunting license.

REVIEW

Add the necessary punctuation to the following sentences.

(chicken cooked in wine)

☐ *The French restaurant on Spruce Street serves excellent coq au vin chicken cooked in wine.*

(1) blade assembly, (2) motor shaft, (3) cowl, and (4) handle

☐ *Before starting to assemble the mower, identify the following parts: 1 blade assembly 2 motor shaft 3 cowl and 4 handle.*

(p. 14)   (p. 16)

☐ *The chart p. 14 and the accompanying graph p. 16 explain the formulas in lesson 2.*

UNIT 10   PUNCTUATION OF QUOTATIONS

Add the necessary punctuation to the following sentences.

(a) shouted "Hey!" and (b) asked, "May we go?"

(a) *Ed shouted Hey and ducked into the bus.*
(b) *Which one of you asked May we go*

☐ Any direct quotation of the spoken or written words of others that we include in our own writing should be set off with quotation marks (" ").

> *He asked me to come.*
> *He asked me, "Will you come?"*

second   Only the (first, second) sentence contains the direct quotation of a speaker.

☐ Add the punctuation necessary in the following example to show that *China, the giant, is dying* is a direct quotation.

"China   dying"   *China, the giant, is dying, Russell wrote.*

☐ The statement which credits a speaker or writer is set off from the quotation by a comma. Add the comma to this sentence.

asked, "Will   *The senator then asked "Will we spend more?"*

☐ When the quotation precedes the statement identifying the speaker, the comma comes at the end of the quotation:

now," the   *"The nation cannot afford to spend more now " the senator continued.*

☐ If a quotation which is a question ends before the sentence does, we place a question mark inside the end quotation marks and do not also use a comma. Add the question mark here.

ready?" he   *"Will you be ready " he asked.*

☐ Similarly, if a quotation which is an exclamation ends before the sentence does, we place an exclamation mark inside the end quotation marks. Add the exclamation mark to this sentence.

here!" he   *"Come here " he cried.*

□ Add the necessary punctuation to the following sentences.

(a) *now?" he*

(b) *now," I*

    (a) *"You're leaving now " he asked.*

    (b) *"We're leaving now " I said.*

□ If a quotation which is a simple statement comes at the end of a sentence, one period inside, not outside, the quotation marks is enough to indicate the end of the quotation and the sentence both. Add the period to this sentence.

right."

    Then he answered, "We're all right "

□ If we quote an exclamation or a question at the end of a sentence, the question mark or the exclamation mark inside the quotation marks indicates the end of both the quotation and the sentence. Add the necessary punctuation to these sentences.

(a) *here!"*

(b) *merger?"*

    (a) *He shouted, "Get us out of here "*

    (b) *The reporters then asked, "Will the government allow the merger "*

□ Add the necessary punctuation to these sentences.

(a) *can."*

(b) *tomorrow?"*

    (a) *His request was simple: "Please come when you can "*

    (b) *His question was simple: "Can you come tomorrow "*

□ If a quotation which is not a question itself ends a sentence which is a question, the question mark follows the quotation marks. No other punctuation is required. Add the question mark to this sentence.

man"?

    Who said, "Go west, young man"

□ Add the necessary punctuation to these sentences.

(a) *impediments"?*

(b) *ourselves?"*

    (a) *What is this line from: "Let me not to the marriage of true minds admit impediments"*

    (b) *Conrad asked, "Why do we lie to ourselves "*

☐ If a very short quotation fits easily within the context of a sentence, we do not use commas to set it off. Notice, however, that the quotation marks are used as usual.

> Saying "Very good" at the right time will please the child.

is not

A comma (is, is not) required before and after *"Very good."*

☐ If short quotations that fit the context of a sentence are questions or exclamations, we do not set them off with commas; but we do use a question mark or an exclamation mark where appropriate. Complete the punctuation in these sentences.

(a) *Stop!"*
(b) *you?"*

> (a) *He cried "Stop " as I passed him.*
> (b) *Bob heard him ask "Where are you " from the darkened building.*

☐ Although short quotations that fit easily into the sentence do not need to be set off with commas, we should always set off with commas those quotations which interrupt the sentences to which they belong. Add the punctuation to these sentences where necessary.

> (a) *Repeating "By the way " as often as you do makes your speeches sound carelessly organized.*

(b) *way," he said,*
"where

> (b) *"By the way " he said "where were you?"*

Shift, but do not change the punctuation in these sentences where necessary.

(a) *buy?";*
"Nothing."

> (a) *I asked, "What did you buy?;" but she answered, "Nothing".*

(b) *"Sugarplum":*

> (b) *He remembered only this about "Sugarplum:" she was six feet tall and weighed over two hundred pounds.*

(b) *"Amen,"*

> (c) *After whispering "Amen", the devout old woman tottered out of church.*

□ Periods and commas should always be placed inside quotation marks that end a quotation.

"I really think," he said, "that little more can be done."

Here the comma following *think* and the period following

are

done (are, are not) correctly placed.

□ Complete the punctuation of this sentence.

roses," the
wedding."

"These are the roses " the messenger announced, "that were ordered for the wedding "

□ Colons and semicolons, unlike periods and commas, should be placed following the quotation marks that end a quotation. Add the necessary punctuation to these sentences.

(a) report": the

(a) *This is what he called his "true report" the prisoner simply opened the cell door and walked away.*

(b) Help!"; however

(b) *We heard a voice faintly crying "Help!" however, we could see nothing in the dark water.*

□ Shift the punctuation in these sentences where necessary.

(a) morning," he
week."
(b) no"; but

(a) *"I am leaving in the morning", he said, "and I will be in New York City all week".*
(b) *The mayor said quietly, "Oh, no;" but his denials were smiled at by those close to him.*

REVIEW

Add the necessary punctuation to the following sentences.

Margaret then said,
"I'm leaving now";
however,

□ *Margaret then said I'm leaving now however, she stayed two more hours.*

Who asked, "Where
did he go?"

□ *Who asked Where did he go*

He screamed "Ow!"
when I

□ *He screamed Ow when I stepped on his toe.*

Add the necessary punctuation to these sentences. Indicate italics where necessary.

(a) "Hillcrest"
Collected Poems
(b) Mourning Becomes
Electra
The New York Times

(a) E. A. Robinson's poem Hillcrest can be found in his Collected Poems.
(b) The recent revival of Eugene O'Neill's play Mourning Becomes Electra received praise in The New York Times.

☐ Italics are slanted letters. Printed in italics, the title of Shakespeare's tragedy looks like this: *Hamlet*. However, since most typewriters cannot print italics, we italicize a word by underlining it: Hamlet.

Shakespeare's Julius Caesar is based chiefly on Plutarch's Lives.

underlined
(underscored)

To show that the titles in this sentence would be italicized in a printed book, they are _____.

☐ The titles of plays and books are italicized. Indicate the italics in this sentence.

Pamela

Although scorned by many, Pamela, Richardson's first novel, has always had a wide audience.

☐ The titles of magazines and newspapers are also italicized.

Time   Life   The
Wall Street Journal

My father subscribes to Time, Life, and The Wall Street Journal.

☐ Indicate the italics in these sentences.

(a) Pygmalion	(a) Pygmalion, Shaw's fine comedy, was made into
My Fair Lady	a musical called My Fair Lady.
(b) The Status Seek-	(b) The Status Seekers, Vance Packard's appraisal
ers The Atlantic	of American society, was thoughtfully reviewed
Monthly	in The Atlantic Monthly.

☐ Titles of poems, short stories, chapters of books, articles in magazines, and columns in newspapers are not italicized but are set off in quotation marks.

"Fissionable Materials" is the tenth chapter of Gregg's book, Nuclear Physics.

chapter	Here the (chapter, book) title is correctly set off with
book	quotation marks; the (chapter, book) title is italicized.

☐ Titles of separately published or produced works (books, plays, movies, magazines, and newspapers) are italicized. Titles of works which are part of separately published works (poems, short stories, chapters, articles, and news-

quotation   paper columns) are set off with _____ marks.

☐ Mark the titles in this sentence.

"Was Darwin Wrong	Was Darwin Wrong about the Human Brain?,
about the Human	Loren Eiseley's article on evolution, was originally
Brain?"	printed in Harper's.
Harper's	

☐ Mark the titles in this sentence.

In Our Time	In Our Time, Hemingway's first published work,
"Big Two-Hearted	contains such stories as Big Two-Hearted River
River"	and The Three-Day Blow.
"The Three-Day Blow"	

☐ Although the majority of poems are short enough to be published as part of a book, Homer's Iliad and Milton's Paradise Lost are among the many poems long enough to be separately published. As the foregoing sentence shows,

italicize   we _____ the titles of such poems rather than set them off in quotation marks.

198

☐ Mark the titles in this sentence. The first poem mentioned is published separately; the second is not.

The Ring and the Book
"My Last Duchess"

> Robert Browning's The Ring and the Book is in some respects related to his My Last Duchess.

☐ Mark the titles in this sentence. The first poem mentioned is not published separately; the second one is.

"Hasty Pudding"
Rape of the Lock

> Joel Barlow's Hasty Pudding has the same mock-heroic tone as Pope's Rape of the Lock.

☐ Mark the titles in these sentences.

(a) "Spelt from Sibyl's Leaves"
Poems of Gerard Manley Hopkins
(b) "A Hanging"
Shooting an Elephant and Other Stories

> (a) Spelt from Sibyl's Leaves, one of Gerard Manley Hopkins' more important poems, can be found in Poems of Gerard Manley Hopkins.
> (b) A Hanging is the most moving essay in George Orwell's Shooting an Elephant and Other Stories.

REVIEW

Mark the titles appropriately in the following sentences.

"The Enormous Radio"
The New Yorker
The Enormous Radio and Other Stories

> The Enormous Radio, John Cheever's most popular short story, originally appeared in The New Yorker and then was reprinted in his collection titled The Enormous Radio and Other Stories.

Moby-Dick
"Loomings"

☐ The first chapter of Melville's Moby-Dick is called Loomings.

UNIT 12 USING ITALICS TO CONTRAST WORDS IN CONTEXT

Italicize where necessary in these sentences.

(a) <u>dux bellorum</u>

(b) <u>plastic</u>

    (a) One of the earliest written notices of King Arthur refers to him as dux bellorum (general) rather than king.

    (b) The term plastic, now commonly a noun as well as an adjective, refers to material which can be easily shaped or molded.

☐ Whenever we include a particular word to discuss as a word rather than for its usual meaning, we should italicize it.

> Iron may be found almost anywhere in the world.
> *Iron* may be used as noun, an adjective, or a verb.

second

We know that *Iron* is a word being discussed as a word, not a noun referring to a kind of metal, in the (first, second) sentence.

☐   Our word silly descends from a Middle English word that described a person who was prosperous or blessed.
    When I say that she is silly, I do not mean that she is either prosperous or blessed.

first
second

Silly should be italicized in the (first, second) sentence but not in the (first, second) sentence.

☐ Indicate italics where necessary in the following sentences.

(a) <u>Hootenanny</u>

    (a) Hootenanny was first used in 1950 to describe a gathering of folk singers.

    (b) Sophisticated college students seem to enjoy the handclapping and folk singing at a hootenanny.

200

□ Normally we italicize foreign words and phrases to distinguish them from the English words in a sentence.

> We felt that the majority of the Mexican people were muy simpatico.

In this sentence the Spanish phrase *muy simpatico* (very nice) (should, should not) be italicized as it is.

should

□ Many foreign words, such as the French noun *pension* (boarding house), would not be distinguishable from English words identical in spelling but different in meaning. Italicizing such words is often the only way we can show what such words mean. Indicate italics where necessary in this sentence.

pension

> Our pension in Rouen was small but clean.

□ Of course, any foreign word in general use becomes a part of English and is not set off in italics. For instance, the Spanish word *guerrilla* (little war) is now part of English. However, the German word *Weltseele* (worldsoul), although occasionally used by English writers, is not yet part of English. Indicate the necessary italics in these sentences.

(a) Weltseele

> (a) For many, Camus' novels are closest to this age's Weltseele.
> (b) The guerrilla fighters moved down the road behind the armored car.

□ Both of the following sentences contain borrowed foreign words. Italicize where necessary.

(a) Weltanschauung

(b) arroz con pollo

> (a) Philosophers close to the German tradition often speak of their common Weltanschauung.
> (b) Those who dislike Mexican food will change their minds after tasting well-cooked arroz con pollo.

Italicize where necessary in the following sentences.

sophisticated

☐ The word sophisticated has undergone several important changes in meaning during the last five centuries.

sign
signum

☐ The English noun sign comes from the Latin noun signum.

Pinus ponderosa

☐ The larger pine trees, particularly the Pinus ponderosa, are important sources of lumber for home building.

UNIT 13   APOSTROPHES

Correct the punctuation in this sentence where necessary.

don't
children's   it's

I'd like to play golf, but I dont dare; I have to build a foundation for my childrens' swings today, and its already half past ten.

not
would

☐ Certain words we use are made up of two words telescoped together and are called contractions. *Don't* is a contraction of *do* _____; *I'd* is a contraction of *I* _____.

☐ The indication of a contraction is the apostrophe ('). Add the apostrophe to the contractions in this sentence.

We'd   I'll

We d like to go, but I ll be surprised if we can.

☐ Make contractions of the bracketed words in this sentence.

He's
aren't

[He is] _____ *ready, but they [are not]* _____.

☐ Make a contraction of the bracketed words in this sentence.

It's

[It is] _____ *a good idea.*

202

<table>
<tr><td></td><td>☐ The contraction *it's* has a near twin, the possessive pronoun *its*, which does not have an apostrophe. The apostrophe distinguishes the contraction from the possessive form.</td></tr>
</table>

It's time for its feeding.

It's
its

The contraction of *it is* in this sentence is _____; the possessive pronoun is _____.

☐ Add the apostrophe necessary in this sentence.

it's still

Its feeding time is over, but its still hungry.

☐ *Its* is like *their, his, our,* and other forms of pronouns which show possession. These pronoun forms (do, do not) require apostrophes.

do not

☐ Unlike possessive pronouns, possessive nouns are formed by adding an apostrophe and—if the noun is singular—an *s*. *Bob's* is the possessive form of the noun _____.

Bob

☐ Form the possessive of the nouns in brackets.

Tonight's
Robertson's

[Tonight] _____ *paper reports in full [Robertson]* _____ *decision on housing.*

☐ If a noun is plural and ends in *s*, we form the possessive by adding the apostrophe after the *s*: *students', teamsters'.*

The professors' position on the matter was clear.

more than one

We know by the form of the possessive *professors'* that the position referred to was held by (one, more than one) professor.

☐   *This book discusses the [corporation]* _____ *legal problems.*

corporation's
corporations'

If the legal problems discussed are those of only one corporation, the correct form of the bracketed word is _____. If the problems are those of several, the correct form is _____.

men	☐ A few plural nouns do not end in s. *Children* is the plural of *child*, and _____ is the plural of *man*.
men's	☐ The possessive ending of plural nouns which do not end in s is 's, not s'. The possessive of the plural noun *children* is *children's*; the possessive of *men* is _____.
children's	☐ Add the apostrophe necessary in the following sentence. *The childrens party yesterday was a success.*
Men's women's	☐ Add the apostrophes necessary in the following sentence. *Mens shirts button on the opposite side from womens blouses.*

REVIEW

Add apostrophes where necessary in the following sentences.

children's	☐ *The childrens grades are good.*
can't it's warmer	☐ *I cant give the dog its bath until its warmer outside.*
I'd players'	☐ *Id rather not try to sneak in through the players entrance.*

Add the necessary punctuation to this sentence.

Charles' brother-in-law's	*Charles pearl cuff links were a gift he received for being one of the ushers at his brother-in-laws wedding.*

	☐ The possessives of singular nouns ending in s (*Charles, Mr. Rogers, series*) do not require an additional s. An apostrophe by itself will indicate the possessive form (*Charles', Mr. Rogers', series'*). Add the necessary apostrophes to this sentence.
Phyllis' Smiths'	*Phyllis watch fell into the Smiths swimming pool.*

204

□ Some writers prefer to add the *s* with the apostrophe to form the possessives of singular nouns ending in *s* (*Phyllis's, Charles's*). However, the general practice now is to add only the apostrophe to such nouns. Add the apostrophe necessary in this sentence.

James'

> *We left early for James party.*

□ The possessive of hyphenated compound nouns (Commander-in-Chief, sister-in-law) is formed by adding *'s* to the final word whether the compound noun is singular or plural. Notice that the plural of most hyphenated compound nouns is formed by adding *s* to the first word, not the last word, in the compound. Thus the plural of *Commander-in-Chief* is *Commanders-in-Chief*; however, the possessive of the same compound noun is *Commander-in-*

Chief's

_____.

□ The possessive form of the singular *sister-in-law* is *sister-in-law's*; the possessive form of the plural *sisters-in-law* is

sisters-in-law's

_____.

□ Form the possessives of the bracketed nouns to complete this sentence.

brothers-in-law's

> *The [brothers-in-law] _____ car broke down on the way to the wedding, but the [bride-to-be] _____ knowledge of carburetors saved the day.*

bride-to-be's

□ Occasionally we use an entire phrase as a possessive.

> *The man's opinion is lightly regarded.*
> *The man in the street's opinion is lightly regarded.*

In the second sentence the phrase *The _____ _____* has the same function as the possessive *man's* in the first sentence.

man in the street's

□   *The man in the street's opinion is lightly regarded.*

This sentence illustrates that to form a phrasal possessive—a possessive having more than one word—we add *'s* to the (first, last) word in the phrase.

last

□ Form a possessive from the bracketed phrase in this sentence.

The girl in
blue's

    [The girl in blue] _____ *hair is*
    attractively cut.

□ Add the necessary apostrophe to this sentence.

Education's

    The Board of Educations weekly meeting was postponed
    until Friday.

REVIEW

Add the necessary punctuation to the following sentences.

Roberts'
brother-in-law's

□   *The Roberts dog bit my brother-in-laws leg.*

door's

□   *The man next doors garage burned down yesterday.*

sergeant-at-arms'

□   *A sergeant-at-arms duties are few.*

UNIT 14 HYPHENS

Place hyphens where necessary in the following sentence.

middle-aged
four-by-eight
second-class

    The middle aged couple sat in their four by eight cabin in
    the second class section discussing their trip.

□ An important use of the hyphen (-) is to link two or more words that function as a single unit modifying a noun.

    The house was built well.
    The well-built house was a century old.

In the first sentence the words *built* and *well* function separately. But in the second sentence they combine to

house

modify the noun _____.

206

	□ *The salesman talked fast.* *The fast-talking salesman sold us the car.*

hyphen
salesman

In the second sentence the words *fast* and *talking* are joined by a _____ to show that they function as a single unit modifying the noun _____.

□   *The creature had ten legs.*
       The ten legged creature ate the bait.

ten   legged

In the second sentence a hyphen should join the words _____ and _____ that modify together the noun *creature*.

□   *The high flying plane left vapor trails.*
       The plane was flying high above the fog.

first

A hyphen is needed between *high* and *flying* only in the (first, second) sentence.

□ Place a hyphen where needed in the following sentences.

short-cropped

     His hair was cropped short.
     His short cropped hair was bright red.

□ Place hyphens where necessary in the following sentence.

well-kept
dry-cleaning

     The well kept secret concerned the sale of a large dry cleaning chain.

□ A group modifier requiring hyphens may have more than two words.

     A fly-by-night company did the roofing.

company

Here a group modifier consisting of three words, *fly-by-night*, modifies the noun _____.

□   *It was a flash-in-the-pan venture.*

In this sentence the noun *venture* has a group modifier consisting of four words, _____

flash-in-the-pan

_____.

□ Place hyphens where necessary in this sentence.

off-the-shoulders

     She wore an off the shoulders blouse.

under-the-counter	□ Place hyphens where necessary in this sentence. *Careful customers avoid under the counter sales.*
twenty-four one-quarter	Place hyphens where necessary in the following sentence. *The package contained four hundred and fifty nails, twenty four wood screws, and ten one quarter plates.*
is not is	□ Hyphens are often used in compound numbers, those having more than one word when spelled out. For instance, *seventy* (is, is not) a compound number, while *seventy-six* (is, is not).
twenty-four	□ All compound numbers below one hundred are normally joined by hyphens; those above one hundred are not. Add any hyphen needed here. *The twenty four salesmen sold over four thousand cameras.*
one hundred	□ A hyphen is needed in *twenty-four* because it is a compound number below _____.
thirty-seven	□ Place hyphens where needed in this sentence. *Two hundred homes were built on the thirty seven acres.*
Eighty-two	□ Place hyphens where needed in this sentence. *Eighty two members voted for the tax measure; four hundred and fifty voted against it.*
three-quarters	□ Since fractions are compound numbers below one hundred, they also are usually hyphenated. Add any hyphen needed here. *The radius is three quarters of an inch.*
Three-eighths thirty-two	□ Place hyphens where needed here. *Three eighths was the inside diameter of all thirty two lengths of conduit.*

	☐ Remember, only compound numbers below one hundred need hyphens. Place hyphens where needed here.
One-third *thirty-five*	*One third of one hundred and five is thirty five.*
	☐ Place hyphens where needed here.
Three-fourths *twenty-five*	*Three fourths of the two hundred boats here were built more than twenty five years ago.*

REVIEW

Place hyphens where needed here.

off-the-cuff	☐ *The retired admiral had several pointed off the cuff remarks to make.*
Twenty-four *thirty-five* *fifty-nine*	☐ *Twenty four and thirty five is fifty nine.*
seventy-five *second-rate*	☐ *At least half of the seventy five homes were built with second rate fixtures.*
over-the-counter	☐ *All over the counter sales were tallied before the close of the market.*
second-mortgage *low-income*	☐ *Second mortgage costs were said to be the reason for the reduction in the building of low income dwellings.*

UNIT 15   CAPITALIZATION

"A	Capitalize the appropriate words in this sentence. *"a sudden squall," he reported, "threw us off our bearings."*

	☐ We capitalize the first word of every sentence. *the three of us went together.*
The	In this sentence we should capitalize the word _____.

☐ If a sentence contains a quotation, we capitalize the first word in it also. Capitalize the appropriate words in this sentence.

He   *"Wait*   he said, "wait a minute."

☐ If a quoted sentence is broken in the middle, we do not capitalize the first word after the break.

> *"Where were you," the boy asked, "when the fire broke out?"*

should not   In this sentence we (should, should not) capitalize *when*.

☐ Capitalize where necessary in this sentence.

"There   > *"there they were," he said, "looking as though nothing had happened."*

☐ If a break in a quotation comes between two separate sentences, the word beginning the new quoted sentence is, of course, capitalized. Make the necessary changes in this sentence.

"Hey!"   *"Come*   > *"hey!" he shouted, "come see our new home!"*

REVIEW

Capitalize the appropriate words in the following sentences.

To   *"Yes*   ☐ *to this she replied, "yes, I'd love to go"; and all I could*
Swell!"   *think to say was "swell!"*

"There   ☐ *"there we were," he said, "fifty miles west of Acapulco, without a breeze stirring and without a drop of fuel."*

Capitalize where necessary in these sentences.

(a) *There*   (a) *there is no other sergeant like sergeant burns.*
Sergeant Burns
(b) *The Renaissance*   (b) *the renaissance, breaking in abruptly on the christian*
Christian   *traditions of the middle ages, created an upheaval*
Middle Ages   *which still lasts.*

☐ Proper names are the names of individual persons, places, or things. Such names are always capitalized.

The man gave Frank and Bob a ride.

proper

Frank and *Bob* are capitalized in this sentence because they are _____ names.

☐ The names of specific places—cities, states, nations—are also proper names. Capitalize the appropriate words in this sentence.

Duluth, Minnesota

We visited duluth, minnesota last spring.

☐ The names of geographical areas are proper names if they refer to specific locations rather than directions. Thus, we capitalize *south* in *the South* but not in *south of Detroit*. Capitalize the appropriate words in the following sentence.

Central United States

Flying west, we were soon over the central united states.

☐ The names of specific oceans, mountains, lakes, rivers, and other geographical features are also proper names. Capitalize the appropriate words in this sentence.

Sierra Nevada
Mountains
Rocky Mountains

The sierra nevada mountains are west of the rocky mountains.

☐ Capitalize the appropriate words in this sentence.

Minnesota
Mississippi River
Gulf of Mexico
New Orleans

Running south from its origins in minnesota, the mississippi river divides the continent, emptying finally into the gulf of mexico below new orleans.

☐ The names of particular historical ages and events—the Renaissance, the Enlightenment, World War II—are proper names. Capitalize the appropriate words in this sentence.

Boer War   Britain's
South Africa

The boer war established britain's claims in south africa.

☐ Capitalize the appropriate words in this sentence.

Reconstruction Period
Civil War   South

The so-called reconstruction period following the civil war had a profound effect on the history of the south.

☐ The names of the days of the week and the months of the year are proper names. The names of the seasons (*spring, summer, autumn,* and *winter*) are not. Capitalize the appropriate words in this sentence.

Sunday, May 4

Last spring—on sunday, may 4, to be exact—I was promoted to my present position.

☐ Words not usually capitalized—lieutenant, bridge, university—are capitalized if they are part of a proper name. Capitalize the appropriate words in this sentence.

Professor Blake

A professor, who was not identified, secretly nominated professor blake for the position.

☐ Capitalize the appropriate words in this sentence.

University of Kansas
Midwest

In looking over the various school bulletins, Ed decided that the university of kansas offered the best courses in his field of any university in the midwest.

☐ Adjectives based upon proper names are normally capitalized: *Christian (Christ), Roman (Rome), Asian (Asia).* Capitalize the appropriate words in this sentence.

English
Renaissance
University of Indiana

His knowledge of english poetry—particularly the poetry of the renaissance—made him the most popular lecturer at the university of indiana.

☐ Capitalize the appropriate words in this sentence.

Professor Flynn
California
Sixties

When professor flynn moved west to california, he did not realize that the cost of living there had gone up since the sixties.

☐ Capitalize the appropriate words in this sentence.

Far East
Marines
Vietnam War

Henry toured the far east in less than favorable circumstances: he was one of the many marines shipped there during the vietnam war.

Capitalize the appropriate words in the following sentences.

Senator Bundy's
Pacific Coast

☐ The other senators applauded senator bundy's appeal for greater conservation efforts along the pacific coast.

May   Italian Alps

☐ In may of last year we visited the italian alps.

Great Depression

☐ The great depression is misnamed because it was relatively mild when compared with previous depressions.

Capitalize the appropriate words in this sentence.

Someone's
Kitchen   Dinah

Do you know the music to "someone's in the kitchen with dinah"?

☐ The first word of a title—whether of a book, play, short story, poem, song, movie, or other publication or work of art—is always capitalized. The other words in the titles are also capitalized, except for articles (*a, an, the*), prepositions (*for, by, to, with*, etc.), and coordinating conjunctions (*and, but, or, nor*). Capitalize the appropriate words in the title in this sentence.

"The Idea of Order
at Key West"

Wallace Stevens' poem "the idea of order at key west" is unusual in its imagery.

☐ Capitalize the appropriate words of the title in this sentence.

"A Sense of
Movement"

Russell Blair's article on modern music, "a sense of movement," is a useful guide to some of the important contemporary composers.

☐ Capitalize the appropriate words of the title in this sentence.

"The Bride Comes
to Yellow Sky"

Although Stephen Crane was an Easterner, his short stories of the West, particularly "the bride comes to yellow sky," have a strikingly authentic quality.

213

Capitalize the appropriate words in the following sentences.

La Gioconda
The Mona Lisa

☐ *Da Vinci's* la gioconda *is a painting better known in this country as* the mona lisa.

"Black Is the Color of My True Love's Hair"

☐ *An almost forgotten folk song is the traditional "black is the color of my true love's hair."*

"In the Back of the Mind of My Father"

☐ *One of James Roberts' most unusual short stories is called "in the back of the mind of my father."*

INDEX